The Art of Workplace English

The Art of Workplace English

A Curriculum for All Students

Carolyn R. Boiarsky

Boynton/Cook Publishers
HEINEMANN
Portsmouth, NH

Boynton/Cook Publishers, Inc.
A division of Reed Elsevier Inc.
361 Hanover Street
Portsmouth, NH 03801–3912

Offices and agents throughout the world

© 1997 by Carolyn R. Boiarsky

The author and publisher wish to thank those who have generously given permission to reprint borrowed material:

Figures 3–3 and 3–4 from information developed by Ron Blicq, Winnipeg, Manitoba. Reprinted with permission.

Geheime Reichssache memo from *Shoah* by Claude Lanzmann. Copyright © 1985 by Claude Lanzmann. Reprinted by permission of Georges Borchardt, Inc., for the author.

Figure 5–1 from *De Re Metallica* by Georgius Agricola. Translated by Herbert Clark Hoover and Lou Henry Hoover. Copyright © 1950. Reprinted by permission of the publisher, Dover Publications, Inc.

"The Play's the Thing" lesson plan from the Aviation 2010 curriculum was created by the Regional Airport Authority of Louisville and Jefferson County, Inc. Reprinted by permission.

CIP is on file with the Library of Congress.
ISBN: 0–86709–426–5

Editor: Peter R. Stillman
Production: Vicki Kasabian
Cover design: Joni Doherty
Manufacturing: Louise Richardson

Printed in the United States of America on acid-free paper
01 00 99 98 97 ML 1 2 3 4 5

To the faculty at Purdue Calumet, and to my best friend and special friends there, who provided an atmosphere of trust and encouragement in which I could write this book, and who represent the very best in teachers—possessing a sensitivity for their students and a solid theoretical knowledge of their fields, tempered by experience in the world outside the academic community.

Contents

Acknowledgments

I would like to acknowledge my debt to my technical writing students, who have been willing to share their knowledge with me, and whose determination to learn to communicate that knowledge has formed the basis for my philosophy in teaching workplace English.

I would also like to express my gratitude to the many people who took time away from their own work to read this manuscript, and to offer their expertise to ensure that this text contains complete, accurate, and up-to-date information, as well as to provide suggestions to create a readable text: Alan Spanjer, Georgia State University; Emily Thrush, Memphis State University; Jane Hosay, Norfolk, Virginia, Public Schools; Beth Neman, Wilmington College; Janet Jackson, Purdue University Calumet; Eileen Schwartz, Purdue University Calumet; and Vicki Ricciardi, freelance writer, Boston. In addition, my thanks go out to those women of the Purdue Calumet English Department—Marilyn Cleland, Judith Burdan, Sally Merrill, and Julie Hagemann—who brainstormed a title for this book, and to Janet Jackson who came up with the one we used.

Finally, I would like to thank all of those people who submitted the enclosed lesson plans, for their willingness to share their projects with others.

Introduction

When I signed my contract with Boynton/Cook, Peter Stillman, my editor, exhorted me to write a humane book. I have tried to respond to his mandate by selecting Robert Pirsig to lead my quest to fuse the technical with the aesthetic, the workplace with the academy, and the impersonal with the humane. Pirsig contends that we make technical things humane when we become part of what we are doing, when we care about them. And I care very much about this book. If I have written it clearly and if you are reading it with an open mind, I believe we can make a difference in the lives of our students.

We teachers seem to spend little time with the "boilermakers," as one instructor describes them: the girl who will take over her father's landscape business, or the boy who will be the fourth generation to work on the line at Caterpillar. Most of our efforts are devoted to college-prep students, to those in Advanced Placement. Although we talk of inclusion, as a profession we are often inadvertently exclusive. C students, and those in the General or Basic Education track, leave our high schools with little preparation for the world outside. And that world is getting tougher and tougher, with beginning jobs requiring a higher degree of academic skills than ever before.

The 1991 SCANS (Secretary's Commission on Achieving Necessary Skills) Report, and the Report of the Commission on the Skills of the American Workforce, "America's Choice: High Skills or Low Wages" (1990), sound a warning note: If America does not upgrade the skills of its workforce so that it can compete on an international level, everyone's standard of living will be compromised. According to Ira Magaziner and Hillary Rodham Clinton (1992), "If we want to compete more effectively in the global economy, we will have to move to high-performance work organizations....We must mobilize our most vital asset, the skills of our people—not just the skills of the thirty percent who will graduate with baccalaureate degrees from college. We can give our frontline workers (the bank tellers, farm workers, truck drivers, retail clerks, data-entry operators, laborers, and factory workers) much more responsibility, educate them well, and train them to do more highly skilled jobs" (8).

To provide students with the skills they will need to qualify for these jobs, a variety of school-to-work programs have been initiated around the country over the past few years. Many of these programs emphasize methods that are more consistent with the learning styles of these students. They also focus on content that is more relevant than the traditional curriculum. An added bonus of these programs is that students not only acquire necessary skills, but they are more motivated to learn and to achieve higher grades. For those of us who are teachers, these new programs mean new lesson plans and more time spent coordinating activities with vocational and business teachers, community leaders, and industry managers. But they also mean classes become less frustrating, more rewarding, and enjoyable.

The Art of Workplace English blends theory and practice to present a picture of how the teaching of workplace English can create a lively, challenging, and satisfying classroom experience for both teachers and students. The book is written to help students prepare for work in the twenty-first century. It presents a picture of the new workplace, and suggests the kinds of knowledge and processes students will need to master in order to communicate effectively in it. Rather than replacing the present English curriculum, the book recommends expanding it. It delineates the methods and activities for classroom use that enable students to be successful in achieving the objectives of this newly extended curriculum.

One

Why an English for the Workplace?

The Buddha, the Godhead, resides quite as comfortably in the circuits of a digital computer or the gears of a cycle transmission as he does at the top of a mountain or in the petals of a flower....The study of the art of motorcycle maintenance is really a miniature study of the art of rationality itself. Working on a motorcycle, working well, caring, is to become part of a process, to achieve an inner peace of mind.

(Pirsig 1976, 18)

For many of us who have been trained to teach canonical literature, workplace English may seem as foreign as motorcycle maintenance. But it shouldn't. Workplace English can allow us to communicate about a part of our lives: our work. If it is work that we care about, then being able to communicate about it should allow us to do it well and to fulfill ourselves.

Thomas Crowell, the owner of a successful insurance agency in the town where I live, has found this type of satisfaction. He called me recently, his voice over the telephone sounding deep, sincere, and mature. He was searching for someone to edit a book he had written.

1

"It's everything I know about sales," he said. "I've been fairly successful and I want to pass on what I know. Maybe I can help someone else."

Thomas Crowell cares passionately about the work he has done. Unlike the dualistic mechanics in Pirsig's book who fail to perceive that their indifference to repairing his machine properly reflects on the quality of their own essence, Crowell does not separate what he is from what he has done. Nor is Crowell's pride based on the crass "economic utilitarianism" and "consumerism" that educator Neil Postman (1995) perceives as the present-day goal of education. Crowell's pride is in the quality of the work he has done, rather than in the profits resulting from it. He has been successful while remaining within the ethical boundaries of his profession, and he wants to mentor others to do the same.

It is this form of success for which we are educating our students, all of our students, regardless of whether they are following a Tech-Prep track, a College-Prep track, or a General track. It is a success that encompasses not only the aesthetic and personal aspects of their lives, but also the professional. Workplace English can provide our students with the skills they need to fulfill themselves in their future work. By failing to offer our students help in acquiring skills for the workplace, we are failing to educate a major portion of their essence as human beings.

A class in workplace English does not have to be a watered-down version of the traditional English curriculum, nor does it have to replace a college-prep one; rather, it can build on the traditional program and expand it. To understand why workplace English should be taught in our schools, we must look at the workplace itself. We need to see how today's occupations have changed, so that we can understand why students require a high level of academic skills, including those in reading, writing, listening, speaking, and visualizing, if they are to enter the workforce at more than a minimal level.

A New Corporate Culture

Since the beginning of the Industrial Revolution, the workplace has furnished authors with a turbulent setting for violent, tragic, and pathetic tales. Charles Dickens sets the story of *Hard Times* in an industrial mid-nineteenth century town in England.

> [Coketown] was a town of red brick, or of brick that would have been red if the smoke and ashes had allowed it; but as matters stood it was a town of unnatural red and black like the painted face of a savage. It was a town of machinery and tall chimneys, out of which interminable serpents of smoke trailed themselves forever and ever, and never got uncoiled. It had a black canal in it, and a river that ran

purple with ill-smelling dye, and vast piles of buildings full of windows where there was a rattling and a trembling all day long, and
where the piston of the steam-engine worked monotonously up and
down like the head of an elephant in a state of melancholy madness.
It contained several large streets all very like one another, and many
small streets still more like one another, inhabited by people equally
like one another, who all went in and out at the same hours, with the
same sound upon the same pavements, to do the same work....
([1854] 1981, 45)

The monotony of a Detroit car factory in the mid-twentieth century
serves as the setting for Arthur Hailey's novel, *Wheels*.

Neither pay nor good fringe benefits could change the grim, dispirit-
ing nature of the work. Much of it was physically hard, but the greatest toll was mental—hour after hour, day after day of deadening
monotony. And the nature of their jobs robbed individuals of pride. A
man on a production line lacked a sense of achievement; he never
made a car; he merely made, or put together, pieces—adding a
washer to a bolt, fastening a metal strip, inserting screws. And always
it was the identical washer or strip or screw, over and over and over
and over and over and over and over again, while working conditions—including an overlay of noise—made communication difficult,
friendly association between individuals impossible. As years went
by, many, while hating, endured. Some had mental breakdowns.
Almost no one liked his work....(1971, 21–22)

While these two passages were written over a century apart, they could
have come from the same book. The descriptions of the drab conditions
in the factories and the mind-numbing work are virtually identical. For
well over a hundred years, factory workers throughout the world
labored under conditions that ranged from dead-end to deadly. They
took no pride in the work they did because they never saw how their
small, isolated jobs were part of a larger, complete project. They were
not asked to think about the product; they were not asked to create
quality, only quantity. Sweatshops abounded, in which women worked
twelve-hour days and children as young as five and six performed labo-
rious and often dangerous tasks. Labor unions, child labor laws, and
federal health and safety regulations ameliorated some of the most drastic problems, but they never eliminated the boredom, and they never
gave a purpose to the work. Then, in the 1980s, global competition,
computerization and robotics, and a man named W. Edward Deming
(1988), who introduced a concept called Total Quality Management
(TQM), transformed the workplace and the lives of the workers in it.

TQM is a company-wide approach that involves the cooperation of
all employees to ensure that all phases of a company's operations are
conducted at the highest quality level. Quality implies a continuous

effort to improve a product and the process used to manufacture it. To accomplish this goal, Deming recommended that management allow for informal dialogues between people in various components in a firm, encourage continual learning, and provide a nonthreatening work atmosphere in which employees perceive themselves as vital links in the manufacturing chain. These new approaches have given birth to teamwork within and between divisions in an organization, and created a more flexible, social, and meaningful workplace environment.

Neither Dickens' description of a British mill town, nor Hailey's description of a car factory provides a valid picture of today's manufacturing environment. The monotonous, isolated, and repetitive tasks that once characterized assembly lines have been made obsolete by new computerized machines and robots. At Caterpillar Inc., thirty-five operators used to work at thirty-five machines to turn out a specific type of transmission case. It took these operators from four hours to two days to set up an assembly line for a new product. Today, only one operator is required to operate the four flexible cell-type machines that have replaced the thirty-five single-function ones. It takes that single operator only a few seconds to reprogram these multipurpose machines from one type of case to another.

Industries have not only installed new machinery, they have restructured their management as they adapt new frameworks for running a plant. These new organizational structures, representing a flattening of the management hierarchy, and Deming's philosophy of Total Quality Management, have given employees the power to make decisions and opportunities for initiative and creativity. With fewer managers running larger divisions, many of the decisions previously made by managers are now made by hourly workers. Furthermore, in team situations, workers are often placed on an equal footing with their managers.

The successful manufacturing plant of the 1990s is aesthetically pleasing, dynamic, social, and egalitarian. This description of a plant located in the Carolinas, which appeared in a 1993 newspaper article, is a far cry from those described by Dickens and Hailey:

> Robert and Terry Wiggins ride to work together each day. At the Caterpillar Inc. sign bordered by flowers, they turn left, traveling along the tree-lined drive that takes them to the company's manufacturing plant. They don't pass through guarded gates, and they don't punch a time clock.
>
> Once at work they meet with members of their respective teams and discuss the activities of the previous day, how they can make their jobs more productive and the plant a better place to work.
>
> Each day the teams, consisting of ten to twenty *associates*, meet for five minutes at the beginning of their shift, and once a week they meet for an hour to look at ways to improve operations.

"If we have a problem, during these meetings, we look at it and try to solve it" [Dick Weiss, plant operations manager explains]. (Bouyea 1993, A5)

It is apparent from the reporter's description that far more than just the architecture and landscaping of this manufacturing company have changed. The entire management structure has been redesigned. Today's workers participate as members of a team, responsible for improving production processes, their company's products, services, profits, and the conditions in the workplace. They engage in all of the tasks related to a particular segment of the manufacturing process, rather than a single task. For example, those on the assembly line may also do minor maintenance. Under the traditional system, if a gauge wasn't accurate, the line would have to shut down until a maintenance worker could fix it. Today, workers on the line are allowed to fix the problem themselves. Previously, the supervisor documented the maintenance work in a written report. Now, the workers write it up.

The following letter, sent in 1996 by the management of an electric utility to all employees shortly after the power industry was deregulated and the utilities were placed in direct competition with one another, summarizes the differences between the old and new way of doing business:

> The Ideal Employee SubTask Group [has] develop[ed] a list of "Ideal Employee Attributes" for the employee of five or ten years from now.
>
> We need to develop *integrity, mutual respect,* and *interpersonal skills.*
>
> We need to act as *team players.*
>
> We need to demonstrate *dependability, initiative, commitment, creativity,* and *flexibility.*
>
> We will have to be *results oriented.*

> If we had had to develop a list of target employee attributes for the utility of the past, we might have included such things as "play it safe; conform, never admit mistakes." [The] corporate structure was designed to reinforce these attributes. [The] end result is that our corporate culture, through subtle cues, told new and old employees what behavior was expected of them. And employees shaped their behavior to conform, so they could be successful within the paradigm of the utility company.
>
> *But that paradigm is changing. The rules are changing. And we need to change also.*

Skills for the Workplace

According to the SCANS Report (the Secretary's Commission on Achieving Necessary Skills), for workers to succeed in the economy of the next century, they will need "a well-developed mind, a passion to learn, and the ability to put knowledge to work. [These] are the new keys to the future of our young people, the success of our businesses, and the economic well-being of the nation" (1991, 1). To achieve these goals, SCANS reports that workers will need to acquire the following skills: thinking, problem solving, decision making, self-management, creativity, teamwork, interpersonal communication, information processing, allocation of time and money, and organizational and technological systems and applications.

The problem is that a large percentage of our youth have not mastered these skills by the time they are ready to leave high school. More than half of the nation's young people leave school without the reading, writing, or mathematical skills required to find and hold a job in a "high-performance industry, an industry that has computerized, roboticized, and streamlined its plants and offices" (1991, 27).

Declarative knowledge—The *what* of learning; schemata consisting of concepts and facts, including organizational patterns and genres.

Procedural knowledge—The *how* of learning; schemata consisting of information that tells how to learn.

Jones et al. (1987) specifies that procedural knowledge is composed of skills and strategies. A skill is a "mental activity that can be applied to specific learning tasks"(14), i.e., predicting, summarizing, and mapping. Strategies are "specific procedures or ways of executing a given skill"(15), i.e., using a specific set of summarizing rules, such as (1) determining the existence of a topic sentence, (2) naming lists, and (3) deleting trivial and redundant information.

Ackerman and Perkins (1989) suggest that procedural skills are composed of thinking and symbolic skills. Thinking skills involve decision making and problem solving. These include comparing, classifying, and organizing in terms of cause/effect, and problem/solution. They write, "Symbolic skills are thinking skills of a sort...We do not just think, we think by means of symbolic vehicles, such as words and images" (83). Symbolic skills include concept mapping and keeping logs reflecting ideas related to a topic.

Conditional knowledge—The *when* and *why* of learning; schemata consisting of knowledge of conditions and contexts associated with specific procedures.

By the year 2000, more than two thirds of the jobs in this country will require less than a baccalaureate degree. However, these positions will require a higher level of academic skills than is presently being offered in the basic or general education track, or in the vocational/ technical courses of most high schools (SCANS 1991). Although almost three quarters of the jobs won't require a four-year college degree, a 1992 survey of graduating high school students indicates that about one half still expect to attend four-year colleges and universities (Stern et al. 1995). This means that not only will many students be overeducated for the jobs available to them, but that they will not have the technological skills required to qualify for the jobs that are available. Thus, we not only need to provide general education students with higher academic skills, but we need to provide *all* students with the kinds of skills that the SCANS report indicates are necessary. These must include procedural and contextual as well as content-related skills.

Educators have recently expanded the types of knowledge students need to acquire beyond the traditional content or declarative knowledge to include procedural and contextual knowledge (Jones et al. 1987). Students need procedural and conditional knowledge so they can transfer their skills as they move from one job to another. While the ability to transfer information has always been important, it is becoming increasingly so as economists forecast a trend of sequential careers with most people engaging in approximately five different jobs over their lifetime.

A Communication-Intensive Workplace

The new workplace of the 1990s is communication-intensive. Directly affecting communication in the workplace is the change in the responsibility for problem solving which has been moved from management's shoulders to the shoulders of the entire workforce. This change has proved successful for both employees and management, since the people on the line are usually more knowledgeable about their jobs and the problems they face than are their supervisors. Gone is the old-fashioned suggestion box where employees scribbled recommendations for better lighting or more holidays on bits of paper that were seldom read. Today's workers often receive bonuses for submitting full-blown proposals to enhance their organization's health or safety record, or to increase the company's bottom line. Max Cox, Brent Haynes, and Vic Huntington, members of the maintenance crew for American Electric Power, can point proudly to an innovation in their company that was initiated at their instigation. The new procedure to prevent friction while maintaining the plant's generator saves more than $2,000 in actual costs and $100,000 in hours by not having to shut down the machinery for as long as was previously necessary under the old method. Besides pride in their accomplishments, the three have won a merit award for their idea, they have received a cash bonus, and their innovation was reported in the company's magazine, *Operating Ideas*.

Team dynamics, in addition to employee enfranchisement, has significantly increased the amount of oral and written communication that occurs in today's workplace. Workers at all levels communicate with their peers, with their supervisors, with people in other departments, and with clients and customers. At meetings, hourly workers are as likely to be team leaders as are supervisors. As team leaders, they must engage in a great deal of written communication, including developing agendas, informing members of upcoming meetings through memos or E-mail, taking notes, and writing up and distributing the minutes of the meetings. All team members are responsible for communicating with each other about what they are doing. Before teams, "you could spend four hours on a line and never talk to your neighbor," one hourly worker at a manufacturing plant confided to me. "Now, we're talking to each other about the job all day long."

The kinds of communication in which employees may engage today and the number of documents they write is staggering, especially considering that only a few years ago this kind of communication was done solely by managers. Nine of the employees on the paint line at a Caterpillar plant in Peoria are members of an Internal Certification team. They are responsible for evaluating their sector and for preparing a report for an internal audit. The report requires them to cover such topics as the number of customer complaints and the time required for responding to them. The members responsible for writing the report have become increasingly adept at using word processing and graphics software programs.

The team has also been responsible for developing a manual to document the procedures followed at the five stations of a paint line. The object of the manual is to provide new employees with the procedures they need to do their jobs effectively. The manual even includes color diagrams. Before Connie Happach, a recent hire, ever came on the floor of the plant, she took the manual home and studied it so she could "know what to do" when she began work.

As the two men responsible for the manual were finishing it, they decided videotapes should also be made so workers could see what to do. When they presented the idea at a team meeting, they were given the go-ahead to develop the tapes.

Earlier in the meeting, the chair announced that an internal audit was coming and that letters needed to go to customers (the dealers), requesting them to submit evaluations for the sector. The team discussed whether to send the charts they had prepared out with the letter. In an effort to keep costs down, they decided to send color charts to the dealers, but make black and white copies for themselves.

Thus, within a single meeting, the team had discussed three different forms of written communication: letters of request, a manual, and a training script. They had also discussed the use of graphics to support their written text, including the use of color. And each had made at least one oral presentation relating to a specific area of responsibility.

Manufacturing is not the only area in the nation's economic sector in which people's roles and responsibilities are being altered. Lead nurses have disappeared in many hospitals. Instead, every nurse is responsible for checking the medication and reporting orally and in writing the changes in patients' status. They are also responsible for maintaining each patient's chart, which often involves writing short descriptions of patients' symptoms or reactions to drugs. At Foster-Gallagher, a mail-order company for flower bulbs, customer-service representatives work in teams to provide support for each other. They are encouraged to share the response letters they write to consumers to ensure that all necessary information is included and that spelling and usage errors are eliminated. Banking personnel at First America are being cross-trained for each other's jobs to enable them to assume each other's positions. When one member of a division takes parental leave or becomes sick, another member who has cross-trained for that position can easily fill in without a long delay for training and without the high number of mistakes that often accompanies the learning of new skills. The procedures for carrying out the various responsibilities are written by the employees and updated periodically.

Under Deming's concept of TQM, every employee is responsible for maintaining quality and every employee is empowered to recommend the changes necessary to improve a product line, manufacturing process, or service. For example, Mary Masters, who works on the trim line at the Diamond Star automobile plant in Normal, Illinois, recognized a problem with the installation of the weatherstripping on the doors of the Mitsubishi Galant. Installing the stripping was difficult and it was taking too long. In addition, it was taking a minute longer to install the stripping on the front doors than on the rear doors, creating a time lag for those working on the rear. The twenty-one members who composed the line examined the problem and decided that they needed a better tool than the magic stick they were presently using to tuck the rubber stripping under the metal edges of the door. Mary, who sounds as if she were fresh out of high school though she has passed the half-century mark, asked everyone on her line to think up a solution. In what approximated the Houston brainstorming session regarding the oxygen problems aboard the Apollo 13, Mary's group tried out a variety of jury-rigged tools, including a pizza cutter and a crude roller made from vinyl siding. It was the roller that proved to hold the promise of a solution, and the line asked the maintenance division to produce one. With the new tool in hand, the line was able to reduce the time differentiation between the two doors from sixty seconds to three seconds. In addition, the group was able to cut the installation time by 300 percent; the members of the line could install the doors in less than forty seconds, whereas previously it had taken three to four minutes. The solution earned the line the president's award for the best solution of the year.

"And it was fun besides," Mary commented when she told me about the project, her voice full of enthusiasm for her job. Since initiating this improvement, Mary has been promoted to management. She credits her promotion to her ability to save the company money through such improvements. She also credits it to her leadership skills, which include skills in communication that helped her persuade her group to pitch in and hunt for a solution to the weatherstripping problem and to persuade her management to accept her proposal to change the tooling.

The litigious nature of our present society has also increased workers' communication responsibilities by requiring them to document everything they do in writing. Workers in a manufacturing plant or in an agricultural environment need to know how to write reports because they never know when they may be involved in a legal situation or present at an accident. Workers at Inland Steel watched a man plunge seventy feet to his death. Those who had witnessed the accident were responsible for reporting what they had observed. Nurses, employees in retirement communities, paramedics, police, social workers, etc., must all maintain detailed records of their conversations with clients and patients for legal purposes. TV programs such as *ER* never show what happens after the Emergency Medical Technicians (EMTs) rush their patients into a hospital. In actuality, these EMTs return to the main area of the Emergency Room and fill in reports before they go on another run.

Because of the demands on workers such as nurses, customer service representatives, tellers, and technicians to communicate effectively in the workplace, it is imperative that we help our students become effective communicators. Furthermore, because of the demand for workers with the types of skills outlined in the SCANS report, we need to provide students with techniques in problem solving, interpersonal communication, and collaboration.

Developing a Highly Trained Workforce

Our challenge is to find ways to teach the skills necessary for succeeding in the workplace to students who have traditionally been unwilling to enroll in college-prep classes or who have appeared unable to achieve a high level of academic performance.

Changing Our Attitudes and Methods

We must recognize that many of the students enrolled in the general education track are not there because they are "stupid," as they are often perceived (Carbo 1990), but because the way in which they are being taught does not match the way in which they learn (Kolb 1984). When they are taught with appropriate methodologies, they have little difficulty in learning higher-level academic skills. We have only to look at our own lives to recognize how much our perceptions about these students' abilities are misplaced. While these students may confuse *there* and *their*, they do not confuse the negative and positive wires crisscrossing our residences when, as electricians, they rewire a room for track lighting or fix a socket. And those of us who cannot saw a straight, clean piece of wood usually stand in awe of those we have hired to build the elegantly molded bookcases for our dens which requires some algebra and geometry along with dexterity and artistic insight.

Matching Teaching with Learning Styles

Our perceptions about the intelligence of these students is caused by a limited definition of "intelligence." We usually think of intelligence only in terms of linguistic and mathematical knowledge. However, educators have begun recently to recognize other types of knowledge. Gardner (1983) suggests that people have at least seven intelligences, representing a "broad range of human abilities" that can be seen "working in their lives in a variety of ways...[given] a context-rich and naturalistic setting." He categorizes these intelligences as follows:

1. Linguistic—the capacity to use words effectively, both orally and in writing
2. Logical-Mathematical—the capacity to use numbers effectively and to reason well
3. Spatial—the ability to perceive the visual-spatial world accurately, and to transform those perceptions

4. Bodily-Kinesthetic—the ability to use one's whole body to express ideas and feelings and to use one's hands to produce or transform things

5. Musical—the capacity to perceive, discriminate, transform, and express musical forms

6. Interpersonal—the ability to perceive and make distinctions in the moods, intentions, motivations, and feelings of other people

7. Intrapersonal—the ability to act adaptively on the basis of self-knowledge

He has recently added an eighth, "natural," the ability to recognize flora and fauna and is considering a ninth, "existential," the ability to question (1997).

McCarthy (1990) developed a model based on individual student learning styles and brain dominance processing preferences called the 4MAT System. She characterizes students as being predominantly one of the following four types of learners:

1. Imaginative—perceiving information concretely and processing it reflectively. This style is indicative of right-brain dominance. These learners "struggle to connect the content of schooling with their need to grow and understand their world." (32)

2. Analytic—perceiving information abstractly and processing it reflectively. The style is indicative of left-brain dominance. These students' learning styles tend to coincide with those of the school.

3. Common Sensical—perceiving information abstractly and processing it actively. While the style is indicative of left-brain dominance, these students are often frustrated with school because they need to work on real problems in order to integrate theory with practice.

4. Dynamic—perceiving information concretely and processing it actively. The style is indicative of right-brain dominance. Like common sensical learners, these students are frustrated with school because they need to integrate the information they receive with their experiences and the real world.

People whose hands communicate what their minds think possess high bodily-kinesthetic intelligence. According to Armstrong (1994), general-education students often exhibit strengths in three of the seven types of intelligences that Gardner (1983) categorizes: spatial, bodily-kinesthetic, and interpersonal. These are required for success in such vocations as drafting, the trades/crafts, technology, engineering, health services, and criminal justice.

Yet little, if any, credit is ever given for these intelligences when secondary-school students are assessed. If we consider the amount of thought that goes into the schematics required for electrical wiring or the planning and designing of a bookcase, then it should be apparent that students who can accomplish such work can also engage in higher-order thinking skills. Why then are their grades so low? Why do they avoid these courses?

The answer is that, while many of them are quite capable of acquiring the higher-level skills, they have found school meaningless and learning difficult because their learning styles differ from the predominant teaching style used in most college-prep classes. These students learn best when instruction is presented through "direct actual experience," when it provides for "cooperation and collaboration," and when it requires "high levels of interaction." However, the predominant teaching style in the schools is usually aimed at those who perceive information abstractly, and who process information reflectively (McCarthy 1990). The style used in most schools is reflected in only one of the four categories that compose McCarthy's model of instructional styles. Students whose learning styles fall within one of the other three categories have varying degrees of difficulty in learning. As these students move up through the grades, academic work becomes "more competitive, more independent, more abstract," exactly the opposite of what these students require (Silver quoted in O'Neil 1990, 5–6). Increasingly, they try to avoid these classes, opting for basic or general education ones.

Many of these students, who are often characterized as *at-risk* students, perceive their high school courses as "pointless, nonchallenging, and boring" (Hull 1993, 20) as it was for Bill Schwart. I first met Bill at one of the weekly Internal Certification Team meetings at Caterpillar Inc. Bill had just finished serving as the editor of the manual documenting the procedures for working on the paint line of Caterpillar's D-6 Tractor and was one of those involved in developing the videotape to accompany the manual. Since no one on the team had ever done a training video, he had requested that the human resources department provide a class in developing one.

"Here I am at the age of 52 still learning," he comments, amazed at himself, since he had hated high school so much he had dropped out to join the army. Why did he quit school? He shrugs, the tattoos rippling over the muscles of his arms as he sits with the others of his team, all in T-shirts, around the conference table where they hold their meetings. "The teacher always made me feel like my questions were dumb," he says in an attempt to explain his decision.

When students like Bill can apply the concepts they learn in concrete ways, and when they can work on projects cooperatively in teams or peer groups with other students, they can acquire the same high-level academic skills as their college-prep classmates (Hull 1993).

Because they are being taught according to their learning styles, they are able to use their intelligence strengths rather than their weaknesses to learn (Brandt 1990). A person's learning style is "the intelligences put to work...[l]earning styles are the pragmatic manifestation of intelligences operating in natural contexts" (Armstrong 1994, 13).

While much of the research examining the relationship between students' learning styles and teachers' instructional styles is controversial, many of the results reported thus far appear to indicate that when students' learning styles are matched to teaching styles, students' academic achievement rises. Dunn believes "Students can learn almost any subject matter when they are taught with methods and approaches responsive to their learning style strengths; those same students fail when they are taught in an instructional style dissonant with their strengths" (1990, 18). Dunn's philosophy appears to support Bloom's (1981) concept of mastery learning: Given sufficient time and an appropriate teaching style, all students can achieve mastery.

Although the results of research studies may be questionable, many of us who have used this approach believe we have achieved successful results. Mike is a case in point: As a student in the basic education track in an Appalachian school in West Virginia where I taught many years ago, Mike seldom handed in an assignment. One day, when the class was working on a literature assignment, I found him reading a biography of Michelangelo instead of Steinbeck's *The Pearl*, which I had assigned. Remembering that Mike liked to draw, I began giving him reading materials that were related to his interest and that included a lot of art work. In turn, he began handing in his assignments.

The discrepancy between learning and instructional styles may not only account for many students selecting the general education track, but it may also account for many C students in college-prep courses (adapted from Kolb 1984). Many underachievers might have reached their potential if they had been taught in a more experiential-style classroom. It is possible that late bloomers would have flowered on time if the instructional approach used in their classes had more closely matched their learning styles (Whitmore 1980). However, as O'Neil (1990) points out, the "lack of alternatives to lectures and textbook-based teaching, classroom design, or grouping factors works against underachieving students" (5).

A Deweyesque Curriculum

Over a century ago, John Dewey recognized the need to alter the methodology of the schools to meet the needs of a student popula-

tion that was very similar to the students enrolled in the basic education classes of today. When Dewey wrote *School and Society* in 1899,
economic and social conditions resulting from the nation's industrialization had caused a drastic change in the population attending
schools, especially on the secondary level. The high school student
population was no longer limited to those from wealthy families
who planned to continue their education through college and to
those who planned to enter the ministry. Education was recognized
as a legitimate institution for improving society, and for assimilating
into the industrial workforce those who had migrated from the
nation's rural areas to its urban centers, as well as those who had
emigrated to the United States from many of the Western European
countries. It became evident that all children, not just those who
were college bound, should attend school beyond the elementary
level. Because of the broad range of intellectual interests, experiences, and backgrounds these new students were bringing to their
education, Dewey recognized that the traditional methods of memo-
rization and drill in exercises isolated from meaningful content
would not be effective: "In the great majority of human beings the
distinctively intellectual is not dominant. They have the so-called
practical impulse and disposition....If we were to introduce into educational processes the activities which appeal to those whose dominant interest is to do and to make, we should find the hold of the
school upon its members to be more vital, more prolonged, containing more of culture" (1981, 19).

Dewey proceeded to introduce a new set of concepts for relating
the school to the interests of this new student population. These
methods closely resemble those advocated for upgrading the academic
skills of noncollege-bound students today.

1. Learning is an active, experiential process. Knowing and doing are
   recursive in a Vygotskyian sense. The one shapes the other in a
   continuous, progressive movement. Students do not truly *know* a
   concept until they have attempted to apply it. As they apply it,
   they acquire additional knowledge about it. Unlike the philoso-
   phers before him, Dewey did not perceive a dualistic universe in
   which doing and thinking are dichotomous. Instead, he saw these
   opposing entities as synergistic.

2. Subject matter should be taught within a social context. Because
   men and women act within a social environment, all content
   areas have a social context. If students are to truly learn about the
   content areas, then they need to learn about them in the environment in which they occur.

3. Education is ongoing. It is a constant "reorganizing and restructuring of experience." Students acquire new knowledge by building on the experiences they already have, in an effort to adapt their aims and desires to the situation in which they live and vice versa.

This applied approach to learning underlies the various school-to-work programs that have been initiated around the country over the past few years. These programs make the skills being taught relevant to students by tying academic coursework to vocational courses and to workplace applications. Dewey recognized that "Occupations...furnish the ideal occasions for both sense-training and discipline in intellectual thought. By occupation, I mean a mode of activity on the part of the child which reproduces, or runs parallel to, some form of work carried on in social life....The fundamental point in the psychology of an occupation is that it maintains a balance between the intellectual and the practical phases of experience" (92–93).

Long before Robert Pirsig perceived a synergistic relationship between working on his motorcycle and understanding "the underlying form of the world," John Dewey recognized that work that was good could not be accomplished without intellectual reflection, and that the intellectual life was empty if it was not involved with the community in which it existed: "An occupation is the only thing that balances the distinctive capacity of an individual with his social service. To find out what one is fitted to do and to secure an opportunity to do it is the key to happiness" (308).

A Student-Centered, Activity-Based, Authentic Curriculum

Today's school-to-work programs are built on Dewey's theories. They use a hands-on, project-oriented approach that is contextually based rather than abstract, and that extends beyond the presentation of theories and abstractions to include the "whys and what fors." The classes are experiential, allowing students to explore, discover, and incorporate the meaning and value of what is being learned into their own cognitive world (Hull 1993). Thus, the school-to-work programs focus on *how* a subject is taught which in turn may modify *what* is taught. Evaluations of recently implemented school-to-work programs indicate that when at-risk and underachieving students understand why they are learning various concepts and how these concepts can be used in the workplace, and when they have an opportunity to use these concepts in concrete ways, their achievement scores increase significantly.

At a community college in downstate Illinois where I taught recently, Phyllis, who was majoring in auto mechanics, refused to revise any of her technical writing assignments; she saw no point in it. Then, suddenly, a month before the end of the term, she asked permission to revise all her work. She had recognized the need to learn to write the kinds of documents she was being assigned in the class because one of her friends, who was employed in Caterpillar's engine paint division, had explained to her how good writing would be closely related to her job and to her success on that job. Her friend's division tested different types of paints, and the employees were expected to write an evaluation report after each test. Her friend had been the one selected to write the reports for the division, and she had just received a promotion because of the quality of those reports. Phyllis needed to see the relationship between her world and that of the school's. She needed to know that the concepts she was acquiring were an integral part of the tools she would be manipulating.

If we attempt to teach higher-level academic skills to general education and underachieving students like Phyllis and Mike by using traditional methodologies, they will most likely expend only a minimum of effort to learn, or they may drop out of school altogether. However, if we develop academic courses in which our methodology focuses on their intelligence strengths, and if we vary our instructional styles to match their learning styles, then both basic education students and the underachieving college-prep students may learn far more than they have ever been given the opportunity to do in traditional classrooms. The challenge is to create courses, using these new instructional methodologies, while simultaneously maintaining the essence of a traditional curriculum. To create such a course in English, it is necessary to understand what workplace English is.

An Expanding English Curriculum

Workplace English is the form of communication we use outside the academic classroom. It is the way we communicate the business of society. It is the process "by which society keeps itself going" (Dewey 1981, 10). Workplace English also allows us to communicate with our descendants and our ancestors; not only in the present, but in the future and in the past. Our knowledge today of the procedures for building the Roman aqueducts, for constructing the double-tier arches in the Roman walls, and for tunneling through steep hills comes from a manual written in 27 B.C. by Marcus Vitruvius Pollio.

The purpose of a workplace English curriculum is not to replace traditional English, but rather to extend it by introducing documents used in the workplace, and by providing the literacy skills necessary for reading and writing these documents. When students adapt the skills and strategies they have learned in traditional English to the documents they will read and write after they leave academia, they will acquire competence in writing about topics in the vocational/ technical courses in which they are enrolled, and in the fields in which they will eventually work.

Including far more than the topics covered in the present courses in business English, workplace English is concerned with reading, understanding, interpreting, and evaluating information in technical and scientific fields as well as communicating information about these fields. It is also concerned with the kinds of communication involved in journalism and public relations.

Furthermore, workplace English encompasses the genres used in the workplace, and provides the literacy skills necessary for reading and writing them within context-specific environments. In workplace English, students learn to read and write letters and memoranda, proposals, position papers, patent applications, instructions, documentation, feasibility studies, recommendations, evaluation reports, and environmental impact statements. Visualization is an inherent aspect of workplace English and students learn about layout, the use of graphics, and visual text. Oral communication is important, and students acquire skill in making oral presentations and in the use of media for enhancing these presentations. Finally, technology has become an integral part of today's communication, and students learn to use computers to gather information on the Internet, to disseminate data on the World Wide Web, and to transmit information via fax and E-mail.

A Context-Driven Curriculum

Because writers must take into account the purpose of workplace documents, it is important that students learn how to write them in a context. Such a context-driven curriculum provides an excellent opportunity for integrating English with vocational courses and with local businesses and community organizations.

Workplace English includes reading technical documents as well as writing them. Several contemporary workplace documents should be of interest to students, including the Kemeny report of the nuclear accident at Three Mile Island, and the Environmental Impact Statement regarding the Manhattan African Slave Burial Ground. The memos warning of the possibility of a problem with the space shuttle Challenger demonstrate the causes of communication failures among experts and the consequences of miscommunication.

Traditional literary works can often provide historical perspectives as well as contemporary insights into the workplace. Thus, many of the literary works that have traditionally been included in high school curriculums, such as Dickens' *Hard Times* and Updike's "A & P"can be taught in applied English.

Maintaining Standards

Because students must be able to comprehend, synthesize, summarize, and evaluate the documents they read, as well as use persuasive rhetoric, develop a coherent text, and meet usage and mechanical standards in the documents they write, workplace English can be as demanding as a traditional English course. The difference is that in an applied English course, students have an opportunity to see how the grammar they're learning, the literature they're reading, and the papers they're writing relate to the real world.

Many of the objectives found in the syllabus of a traditional English curriculum apply as much to workplace English as to literary and academic prose. These include learning to write research papers, persuasive discourse, and effective descriptions, and learning to use metaphorical language. Because of the similarities between academic and workplace writing, an assignment requiring students to write a position paper or instructions for operating a VCR can meet the objectives of a traditional English curriculum. Teaching students strategies for writing a position paper strengthens their skills for writing persuasive discourse.

Differences Between Workplace and Traditional English

Perhaps the greatest difference between workplace and academic or literary English involves stylistics. In academic English, sentences and paragraphs are usually long, while in workplace English they are kept short. Workplace English, like academic English, requires that a standard style be used for formatting papers and citing and referencing sources. However, the style differs. In traditional English, the conventions of style are established by the style guide of the Modern Language Association, which proscribes the author/page format for citing and referencing sources. Workplace English, however, uses either the number style of the theoretical sciences or the author/date style of the applied sciences.

Differences also exist between the way workplace documents and literary works are read. Students have been taught to engage in close reading of a literary text, to read from the beginning to the end of a story or poem, to read behind the lines, to consider each word in a text as part of the whole. But workplace documents can and should be read in a variety of ways. Depending on the reader's purpose, workplace documents may be scanned, skimmed, searched, studied, or evaluated (Huckin 1983).

Conclusion

In the following two chapters, I will examine the kinds of communication that occur in the workplace and the specific written documents and oral forms that this communication takes, and I will describe the methods and activities that can be used in the classroom for teaching these. In Chapter 4, I will look specifically at fusing the traditional English literary curriculum with this new aspect of English, to ensure that we achieve the objective of Tech Prep: *to strengthen students' academic skills*. In Chapter 5, I will suggest ways to use the technology of the twenty-first century for enhancing instruction as well as preparing students to use this technology. Finally, in Chapter 6, I will recommend ways to integrate the English curriculum by collaborating with other sectors of the school and community to create an authentic, exciting, and challenging curriculum for all students.

By extending the traditional curriculum to encompass workplace English, we have an opportunity to reach many students whom we have been unable to reach previously. We also have an opportunity to help *all* students become better able to communicate in the new global society in which they live. If we can willingly learn something about motorcycle maintenance, then perhaps we can help our students learn the essence of Zen.

Two

Methods for Teaching the Genres of Workplace English

Because of the changes in the workplace discussed in Chapter 1, the present decade marks the first time since the industrial revolution began that employees have had a voice in the workplace. Opportunities for communicating concerns and ideas have given workers confidence in their own capabilities and provided them with new paths for moving ahead in their careers.

David works at a plant where steel molds are made for the plastics industry. Recognizing the need to upgrade his skills in order to hold onto the job he had, he enrolled as a nontraditional student in a two-year degree program in information systems and computer programming at the local university where I teach. Like many of the other students at this college, David alternated between work and school. Working the early shift, he attended classes during late afternoon and early evening, spending nights and weekends studying. He was a quiet man, thin and angular, about 32, with the kind of straight brown hair that never sets quite right. He'd sit in the back of my technical writing class, nervously fidgeting with a pencil as he tried to learn whatever I was saying about conventions and audience analysis. Like so many other technical students who had had only limited success in previous English classes, he was uncomfortable in this class, unsure of himself. I figured he was probably like that at his work also, quiet, unprepossessing. One day while on the job, David noticed that one of the machines was not being used to its maximum capacity and decided to write a proposal recommending a way to make it more efficient. His supervisor liked the idea and approved it. Shortly after that, David was asked to work on a plan to improve another aspect of the division.

"My boss changed his view of me after I researched an idea and presented it effectively," David wrote to me. "It [my proposal] has been a turning point in my career." I could see the look of pride in his eyes and hear, as he wrote those words, a new surge of confidence in his own worth.

David had found his workplace voice. If other employees are to experience the same success, they need to acquire specific knowledge and skills in workplace communication so that they, too, can use their voices to express their ideas effectively.

Communication in the Workplace

To determine which documents students need to learn to write and the skills they need to acquire to write them, I spent the eighteen months prior to writing this book visiting various industries and businesses, learning about the types of jobs held by people with two-year college degrees, and discovering the kinds of communication in which these people are now engaged. In major cities in the Midwest, I met with people in the steel industry and in heavy equipment manufacturing, in the automobile and motorcycle industries, and in construction technology. In rural areas I talked to people in farm and seed production, and in animal husbandry. As I traveled across the country, I met men and women involved in nursing and radiography, doing long-term nursing care and working on emergency medical teams. I spoke with people engaged in police work and working with the FBI special forces. I visited businesses engaged in consumer services, in duplicating and printing, and in retail sales. I talked with bank managers, railroad administrators, and computer systems managers. All indicated that no matter what the job, today's workers needed to be able to communicate effectively both orally and in writing. Often they showed me the various documents for which their workers were responsible. I found that while workers may be in very different sectors of the economy, ranging from health services to manufacturing, from agriculture to criminal justice, they are engaged in reading and writing many of the same kinds of documents: memoranda, logs, instructions, management documents, procedures, proposals, minutes to meetings, and progress and evaluation reports.

All of the documents that I saw during my visits were short. The readers were busy people with limited amounts of time. They wanted to get the information they needed as quickly and easily as possible.

Often they scanned the documents, searching for specific data to help them make a decision. They seldom read an entire text.

Skill Needs

During my discussions at the various industries, managers impressed on me time and again that their employees' major difficulty in writing was in presenting information fully and accurately within a limited space. It became evident that students must not only learn to write the various types of documents, but that they need to learn new procedural and contextual skills. These include synthesizing information so that it is presented concisely, differentiating between necessary and irrelevant data, acquiring effective observation and interviewing strategies for gathering data so that reports are complete, and learning the text grammars for truncated sentences so that notes can be understood clearly.

Managers almost always added that they were concerned with employees' poor spelling of both the technical terms of their field and of common terminology. Many of the documents the employees wrote, especially the logs, were seen by a large number of readers, especially when legal proceedings were involved. Regardless of employees' knowledge of their field, spelling errors left readers with the impression that writers were careless and lacking in competence, not only in spelling but in their content areas. Often these errors resulted from writers' failures to proofread and revise their logs. Most workers write or enter their logs into their computers as first drafts. Because they seldom have time to engage in the revision phase of the writing process and the documents don't go through a review process, errors are usually not caught before the documents are released. I became convinced that students need practice in timed writing and proofreading for correct spelling and usage.

My findings are supported by the SCANS report (1991). After studying five major career clusters—manufacturing, health services, office services, retail trades, and accommodations and food services, SCANS found a set of common competencies and skills shared by all workers. Based on the results of this study, the SCANS report outlines the following communication skills that students need to acquire if they are to communicate successfully in the workplace.

> Reading—Locate, understand, and interpret written information in prose documents—manuals, graphs, and schedules—to perform tasks; learn from text by determining the main idea or essential message; identify relevant details, facts, and specifications; infer or locate the meaning of unknown or technical vocabulary; and judge

the accuracy, appropriateness, style, and plausibility of reports, proposals, or theories of other writers.

Writing—Communicate thoughts, ideas, information, and messages in writing; record information completely and accurately; compose and create documents, such as letters, directions, manuals, reports, proposals, graphs, and flow charts; use language, style, organization, and format appropriate to the subject matter, purpose, and audience; include supporting documentation and attend to level of detail; check, edit, and revise for correct information, appropriate emphasis, form, grammar, spelling, and punctuation.

Listening—Receive, attend to, interpret, and respond to verbal messages and other cues such as body language in ways that are appropriate to the purpose.

Speaking—Organize ideas and communicate oral messages appropriate to listeners and situations; participate in conversation, discussion, and group presentations; select an appropriate medium for conveying a message; use verbal language and other cues, such as body language, appropriate in style, tone, and level of complexity to the audience and the occasion; speak clearly and communicate a message; understand and respond to listener feedback; ask questions when needed.

By helping students acquire these skills, we can help them develop their workplace voice, a voice that speaks with a tone of authority and confidence.

Effective Methods for Teaching Workplace Genres

As we discussed in Chapter 1, the majority of students enrolled in applied English courses learn best through a hands-on, project-oriented, experiential approach which involves collaboration. Those teachers who are using a process approach in the teaching of reading and writing, who incorporate reader response in their literature lessons, and who use small groups as part of their classroom management structure are already implementing many of the methods that facilitate learning among these students.

Two methods specifically related to applied English need to be added to the methods already being implemented as part of the process approach. These involve following a developmental model that provides students with a scaffold on which to climb, and teaching within a realistic context.

Following A Developmental Model

While students may have developed some maturity in terms of reading and writing literary prose, they are still at a very early stage in their knowledge of workplace prose. Most have had no instruction in it, nor have they had opportunities to interact with it. In most cases, we don't introduce students to workplace documents until they are in high school and at a late stage in their educational development. However, it is important to recognize that they are at a very early stage of their development in workplace literacy. Therefore, we need to begin our instruction in workplace genres from what is equivalent to the preschool stage of literacy. We need to begin by helping students acquire story schemas and cognitive clarity. And we need to use the same strategies that we use to teach students new literary genres, including constructing a scaffold to support students as they learn new concepts by building on prior knowledge, moving from simple to complex problems and schemas, and introducing the conventions of various genres and subgenres.

Developing Schemata. According to research, children need to acquire story schemas if they are to learn to write. Mikey told the following story to his teddy bear when he was four years old:

> Once upon a time there was a billy goat, and he ran out of toothpaste. He went to his friends and showed them his teeth.
> "Boy, we won't play with you because you have too dirty teeth." And he went out to the store and got some toothpaste.
> "Boy, you have nice clean teeth and now we'll play with you."
> And that's the end.

Mikey's tale demonstrates a knowledge of the story schema for fairy tales. There is a conventional opening (once upon a time). The story has a beginning, middle, and end. There is a plot in which a character has to overcome a problem. And there is a happy conclusion to the story.

By the time many children begin school, they have acquired schema for a variety of literary genres, including fables and nursery rhymes. Children who come from homes where parents read to them have often learned the schemata so well that they can create their own stories, as Mikey did. Young children develop story schemata by hearing, and later reading, many stories, plays, and poems. As they matriculate through school, their repertoire of literary texts is expanded as they are introduced to a wide range of reading materials. By the time they are in secondary school, they have acquired schemata for a large number of genres and subgenres, including dramas, limericks, ballads, novels, short stories, essays, and nonfiction. Most students also acquire schemata for such social genres as bread-and-butter thank-you notes for holiday presents and invitations for parties.

While our secondary students come to us with this broad knowledge of literary texts, few have any knowledge of the texts that are written outside the academic world. As a result, very few students have acquired schemata for the workplace documents they will eventually be expected to read and write. In addition, they do not have any perception of the context in which these documents are written or read. They seldom have an opportunity to watch their parents write at work, or to read the documents their parents read for their jobs. In addition, because of the kinds of work teenagers are usually hired to do, few are required to read any document beyond a training manual they may have had to study for their job, nor have many seen their supervisors engage in writing on the job.

To develop schemata for the genres of the workplace, secondary students should be introduced to various documents in the same way that they are introduced to such sophisticated and unfamiliar literary subgenres as sonnets and odes. Just as we usually require that students read several Shakespearean sonnets before we ask them to try to write one, we must provide students with the opportunity to read the kinds of workplace documents they will eventually write.

But it is not enough simply to assign readings to students. Their assignments need to be structured so that they read the various texts in order to learn how to write them. They must "read as writers" (Smith 1984). Students are used to reading to obtain *content* information. However, in reading to learn how these documents are *written*, the text is as important as the content. Students need to examine the texts to discover the organizational patterns, focus, style, and vocabulary of the various documents, and they need to consider how writers take their audiences and purposes into consideration. When a professional writer accepts an assignment to write in a new field or in a new medium, she will typically examine a number of similar documents to determine the conventions for that particular community and document. For example, when I was asked to conduct a training session for engineers who wanted to publish in the *IEEE Transactions*, a prestigious professional journal published by the Institute of Electrical and Electronic Engineers, I studied four or five recent issues of that journal. I discovered that the first sentence of the abstracts was written in passive voice. With this information, I proceeded to develop a module in my session that dealt with the passive voice, how it differed from active voice, and how to write it.

When we give students documents to read, we should specify what we want them to study. For example, we may ask them to look at the organizational pattern, or the use of visual text and graphics. Once they have read the texts, we need to discuss their findings to make the knowledge they have gained about writing overt; i.e., charts and tables are included, headings and subheadings are used. Discussions about their findings are not sufficient. We must also help students become aware of the procedures they used to discover the conventions of a particular type of document, so that when they are assigned to write in an unfamiliar genre, they can derive the appropriate conventions. To become aware of the heuristics and procedures they used, they must engage in metacognition (Campione 1987).

Marzano et al. (1988) describe metacognition as "being aware of our thinking as we perform specific tasks, and then using this awareness to control what we are doing...metacognition involves two primary aspects: knowledge and control of self and knowledge and control of process" (9–10). Jones et al. (1987) build on this premise, stating that "learning is strategic in that model learners are aware of and control their efforts to use particular skills and strategies....Awareness refers not only to knowledge of specific cognitive strategies, but also to knowledge of how to use them and when they should be used. Control refers, in part, to the capability to monitor and direct the success of the task at hand" (15).

Through metacognition, students can begin to internalize their strategies, i.e., looking at a page to see how the writer has presented lists and statistical findings, examining the degree of detail included in a report for a given audience, etc. Through metacognition, we can ensure that students recognize the procedural knowledge they gain, so that they can transfer that knowledge to other tasks (Jones et al. 1987).

Two of the most effective ways to help students internalize strategies is through modeling and scaffolding. In modeling, the teacher demonstrates aloud her thinking processes in working through a problem. Scaffolding involves supporting students' attempts to use a skill by providing additional instruction, visual prompts, and graphic representations, and by modeling. The scaffolding can be organized in several ways, including the following:

1. Begin at the students' level and increase demands gradually.
2. Provide the maximum support needed by the students, and then gradually fade out the support as students acquire mastery (Jones et al. 1987, 54–55).

According to Frank Smith (1984), "Children will read stories, poems, and letters differently when they see these texts as things they, themselves, could produce" (54). It is not until students learn to apply strategies related to written communicaton across a broad spectrum of tasks that they become part of a community of writers, or, "members of the club."

> When teachers inform their students about: (1) what strategy they were learning, (2) how they should employ the strategy, and (3) in what context they should employ the strategy, the students indicated greater awareness of what they were learning and why. In addition, these students performed better on achievement measures than did students whose teacher did not fully inform them regarding these aspects of strategy use. (Jones et al. 1987, 53–54)

Developing Cognitive Clarity. Cognitive clarity refers to understanding how texts are read. Young children whose parents read to them acquire cognitive clarity, which involves understanding that we read from left to right, from top to bottom, and that we read each word, line by line, page by page. Young children also acquire cognitive clarity by watching adults involved in reading. They perceive that literary texts are read in the home for enjoyment, that each page is read, that the book is read from cover to cover, and that the books often involve some analysis and discussion. If children observe their parents reading their mail, they perceive that invitations and letters from friends are read with enjoyment, while bills and advertisements are scanned with annoyance. And if they watch their parents correspond via E-mail, they become familiar with that genre.

Students need to develop cognitive clarity in order to read workplace documents effectively as well as to write them appropriately. Cognitive clarity in workplace literacy involves understanding that documents are read piecemeal, not in their entirety; that they are read to acquire specific information; and that they may be skimmed, scanned, or searched rather than read closely, word by word, page by page.

One way we can help students acquire cognitive clarity for workplace texts is to provide them with textbooks that include case studies indicating how readers handle documents. Couture and Goldstein (1985) present cases that are typical of workplace situations, while Boiarsky and Soven (1995) present unique cases that have become classics in the study of workplace communication, such as the space shuttle Challenger disaster, the Three Mile Island nuclear accident, and the Chicago flood. Discussions of the cases in both books can provide students with an understanding of how workplace documents are influenced by the contexts in which they occur, thus helping students acquire the contextual knowledge discussed by Marzano et al. (1988) and Jones et al. (1987). The documents in Boiarsky and Soven's book can help students become aware of the importance of readers' responses to a text, one of the major concepts students must understand in learning workplace English. In this book, students not only read a memo, but they read the responses to that memo, which offer them insights into readers' interpretation of a text. Thus, by reading a NASA manager's response to a memo relating to problems with the Challenger space shuttle, students discover that the manager failed to understand the original message from the Morton Thiokol engineer. Because they are aware of the portentous consequences of that miscommunication, they come to recognize the importance of considering the reader in workplace writing.

Perhaps a more effective method than assigning students to read textbooks is that of engaging them in role plays, in which they are required to read documents under a variety of experiences simulating a workplace environment. In an assignment to write instructions for a software program, students may assume the role of users and write the instructions and graphics for actual use in their computer labs. In another situation, students may write proposals suggesting changes in their institution. They can then swap papers and, assuming the role of administrators, read the proposals to decide whether or not to approve the suggestions.

Finally, speakers from industry can talk to students about how they read and write documents at their jobs. Representatives from local companies or students' parents may be willing to visit classes and talk about how the documents they read and write at work are developed and used. Students can also interview their parents about how documents are written at their workplace and under what conditions and by whom they are read. They can then share this knowledge with each other by writing a brief description of the context of each document and then compiling these into a booklet that can be placed on a table in the classroom for everyone to read during a time set aside for that purpose. In a variation, instead of writing a description, students can share the information orally in small groups or in brief class presentations.

Building on Prior Knowledge. The best way to introduce students to workplace documents is to build on their prior knowledge by beginning with genres that are fairly close to those with which they are familiar. Because most students have had experience with letters related to social situations, correspondence related to the workplace is a good starting point. It is fairly easy to move students from the conventions of a social letter, which requires a salutation, closing, and signature, to the conventions of a business letter, which adds such things as the address of the writer, the date, the heading for the addressee, and a subject line. From business letters, it is not too difficult to introduce memoranda and such electronic correspondence as E-mail and fax.

A second genre with which most students are familiar is that of instructions. Most have either cooked from a recipe, used the schematics of a Lego set, or followed directions to put together an unassembled product. Many have also used either on-line or hard copy documentation to run a software program.

Another genre with which students have acquired some acquaintance is templates. By high school most students have filled out one or more forms. Many have applied for jobs; some have acquired a driver's license; and others have filled out some sort of medical form.

Moving from Simple to Complex. It is always good to begin with a task that is simple and requires few steps. Such a task gives students the opportunity to master the basic conventions, style, and format of a genre, before they have to tackle a complex problem. For example, you might ask students to write a set of instructions for such simple tasks as using a bagel cutter, egg splitter, or egg beater before asking them to write instructions for using a Cuisinart, espresso maker, or Salad Shooter.

Introducing the Conventions. A myth is circulating in academia that if we give students the conventions, if we tell them how to organize their information, how to write openings and closings, we are detracting from their creativity. Far from it. In fact, we are increasing their opportunities to be creative.

Conventions are the accepted "practice, style, or structure" of a text; for example, invoking the blessings of a deity or muse in epics; using alliteration rather than rhyme in Anglo-Saxon poetry; or including a pair of minor as well as major lovers in most comedies (Lazarus and Smith 1983).

By providing students with the framework for their documents, we free them to focus on the content of their message, the interior text. And it is the content of the message that is of prime importance in workplace documents. In addition, if we reflect on how we teach new literary genres, we will recognize that we provide students with the conventions before they ever start writing. We usually begin a unit on the Shakespearean sonnet by lecturing on the form, explaining that it is composed of fourteen lines that are divided into an octave and a sestet, the octave often setting forth a problem and the sestet providing a solution. We also discuss the rhyme scheme and meter and provide a summary of the kinds of topics usually written about. Since we do not think that giving students these conventions detracts from their creativity in writing a sonnet, I don't believe giving them the conventions for a particular subgenre in workplace literature will be conducive to formulaic writing either. For example, in writing a set of job procedures, employees need to know that the conventions include establishing hierarchies of information, listing items, using bullets to identify items and spacing to separate items, and using passive voice. Once they know the conventions, students can focus on the information they plan to communicate, and on determining the best way to express that information.

Students can learn the conventions for workplace English in several ways. One is to teach the conventions inductively, by providing students with a large number of documents that fall within a specific subgenre and asking them to determine the conventions of that subgenre by comparing the texts and defining the common elements across the examples. By reading and examining these documents, students can acquire the conventions as well as begin to understand how situation influences the way documents are written in the workplace.

For example, students might be given six or seven examples of letters of request for which the context is known and asked to note the similarities and differences. As they examine the various examples, they might perceive that most salutations use the "Dear...," but that some address the person by the last name, while others use the first name and a few don't use the salutation at all. They might also notice that closings differ, ranging from "Yours truly," or "Truly yours," to "Sincerely," "Respectfully," "Cordially," or "Regards." Deviations such as these provide an opportunity to relate the style of the letter to its context.

The second method for instructing students in the conventions of various workplace genres is more direct. Using this method, the teacher either assigns a chapter in a textbook, distributes a handout, or outlines the conventions of a specific subgenre. I use both methods because I like students to examine several examples, to get a feel for the genre. Of the two, the direct method saves time and effort, which can be used in learning how and where to gather information or drafting an effective message.

Conventions are as necessary to readers as they are to writers. They allow readers to predict accurately what they will read. They also facilitate fluent reading. For example, readers know that, according to the conventions, the name of a writer will be listed at the top left side of a memo and that a brief statement about the subject will be written slightly below it. Therefore, they know to look in the upper left corner of the message to learn who has sent them a document, and to look slightly below the name to discover the topic to be discussed so that they can decide whether to read the message immediately, put it aside to be studied later when they have more time, or pitch it into the wastebasket. If the information is not placed where convention designates it, readers become confused.

In more complex documents, conventions help readers follow the logic of a text. Just as the readers of a fairy tale know that, after the princess is cast under a spell, the prince will come and free her from it, readers of a proposal know that, after a problem has been described, the writer will suggest a solution. When the convention is not followed, readers do not read what they have predicted, and they become frustrated.

Conventions not only help readers navigate a text, they also help writers organize their information appropriately. If writers know that the conventions of a proposal require that it follow a problem/solution organizational pattern, and that the information in each section should follow a most-to-least-important sequence, then writers know how to organize and sequence their information.

Using A Contextual Approach

A contextual approach involves hands-on, collaborative projects that require students to engage in problem-solving activities in either a simulated or actual situation. As students participate in the activities, they learn the genres that are involved and acquire the skills necessary to engage in them successfully.

More than ten years of teaching have convinced me that teaching in context offers the best approach for helping students acquire the skills necessary for the workplace. First, such an approach is experiential and project-oriented, and therefore closely matches students' learning styles and intellectual strengths (Kolb 1984). Second, it facilitates students' learning how situation, audience, and purpose affect communication. Finally, it allows for the simultaneous introduction of a number of mechanical skills which, because they are taught in context, can be easily acquired (Calkins 1980).

In using this approach, the teacher serves as a curriculum developer and facilitator whose task involves developing projects that revolve around the genres and skills the students need to learn. For example, for students to learn to write instructions, I develop an assignment around a situation that requires students to write a set of instructions that can actually be used.

Developing a project assignment can be one of the most challenging—but also one of the most enjoyable—aspects of teaching; certainly it is one of the most creative. Such projects need to be locally oriented and directly related to students' needs or interests if they are to elicit student involvement. Opportunities for projects often exist in the businesses, industries, and nonprofit organizations within your community and in your school. A high school in Illinois solicits desktop publishing projects from local businesses. Another Illinois high school works with a community college on a series of projects related to an electric car donated by Chrysler Corporation. My business writing students recently conducted a needs assessment to learn students' needs in the computer labs.

Student-Centered Activities. Many genres and subgenres can be integrated into a student-centered curriculum (Moffett and Wagner 1992). For example, if students are complaining about something in the school, you can use the opportunity to present a lesson on writing a letter of complaint. If students want the administration to change something, like bringing fast foods into the cafeteria or implementing a special dress day, you have an opportunity to teach the writing of persuasive correspondence or a proposal for change. In addition, a controversy related to administrative issues can open the door for a lesson on writing a white paper or an information report. At Munster High School in Indiana, the school board was debating whether or not to eliminate class rank. Mary Yorke, an English teacher, discovered that by requiring students to assume the role of the principal and make a presentation to the school board either favoring or opposing the idea, she could effectively present the concept of writing for an audience. "It was the first time I ever really knew I had gotten across the idea of writing for an audience and a purpose," she admitted to me one day.

Integrating English and Technical/Vocational Courses. Perhaps the best way to motivate students who are enrolled in a technical/vocational track is to coordinate assignments with their content courses, so that the students perceive the writing they do as an integral part of their content work rather than as an additional writing assignment whose audience is the teacher and whose purpose is a grade, regardless of the scenario provided.

In the electric car project, community college students enrolled in a mechanical technology course redesigned the car that Chrysler had donated. The project was carried through several semesters. In the process, students were required to engage in writing a variety of workplace documents, including specifications for fabricating and installing the various parts that had been redesigned, a vehicle operations manual, instructions for charging the battery, periodic progress reports, a final report when the project was completed, memos announcing advisory committee meetings, and letters thanking members of the advisory committee for attending the meetings. The students were also responsible for making a brief oral presentation to the advisory committee on their progress.

During one phase of the project, the vehicle was presented to local high school students enrolled in an auto technology course. The high school students' task was to reassemble the car, based on the designs and specifications prepared by the community college students. There was considerable oral discussion back and forth between the two classes as the high school students questioned the specifications. The high school students then engaged in written communication as they made changes to the specs in order to clarify the problems they had encountered in reading them. The result was that the college students discovered how readers read specifications, a discovery which in turn caused them to realize that they needed to write more explicitly. The high school students learned how to read specs in terms of understanding and evaluating them, to ask questions to get the answers they needed, and to edit, revise, and write their own specifications.

Conclusion

By introducing our students to various written genres and subgenres, and by providing them with instruction in the skills and strategies they will need to read and write them, we can help them find their workplace voice. We can help them exercise their voices judiciously and effectively by using real-life scenarios and projects in combination with student-centered and structured activities that engage students in reading and writing workplace documents, and by offering them opportunities to practice listening and to present their own ideas on a variety of issues.

Chapter 3 provides an explanation and discussion of the major genres and subgenres that employees with associate degrees will be expected to write in the workplace. Each of these can be taught by using the methods we have discussed in this chapter.

Three

The Genres of Workplace English

We have spent a great deal of time in our traditional English classes helping students develop their literary and academic voices. We have helped them enhance their fluency so that their ideas unfold in long, flowing sentences. We have encouraged them to use adjectives and adverbs to enhance their descriptions, and we have urged them to include often minute details to provide a complete picture in words. But here's the rub: To write for the workplace, employees need to eliminate unnecessary details; sentences and paragraphs need to be short; and messages should be reduced to their essence, providing only the esssential information.

This chapter provides the audience, purpose, conventions, styles, and formats of various genres and subgenres of workplace prose. It also provides suggestions for activities related to teaching these prose forms and lists the skills students will need for writing them effectively. However, the chapter does not provide detailed descriptions of the various documents. These can be found in the many professional, technical, and business writing textbooks on the market. This chapter should be used to help you decide which workplace documents to teach. Once you have made that decision, you should turn to one of the textbooks.

The Conventions of Workplace English

We need to help students learn the conventions, styles, and formats used in workplace prose, just as we helped them acquire the skills for

Figure 3–1

Example: Academic Prose—There are several major differences between the conventions used for academic prose and those used in workplace prose. Perhaps the most obvious is the length of the paragraphs and sentences. Another obvious difference is the way in which items are listed. Still another difference is the use of technical terminology. Finally, there is the difference in the use of graphics and visual text.

Example: Workplace Prose—There are several major differences between the conventions used for academic prose and those used in workplace prose. These differences involve the following aspects of written text:

- length of paragraphs and sentences
- listing of items
- use of technical terminology
- use of graphics and visual text

---

literary and academic texts. We need to help them recognize the differences between these various types of prose and when to use each. For example, in academic and literary prose, lists of items are written as part of a paragraph and transitions are used to indicate the relationship between them. But in workplace texts, items are listed vertically and separated by bullets or numbers (see Figure 3–1).

Sharon Arbiture, an English teacher at Libertyville High School in Illinois, has developed an activity to help students perceive that these two forms of writing require different conventions. The activity and several student samples follow.

Clarifying the Difference Between Technical and Literary Prose

Literary writing differs from technical/scientific writing in several ways: Literary writing appeals to the imagination and the senses and is suggestive. Technical writing is concise and specific to its purpose to provide information to a reader. A literary description paints a picture, often using images and poetic devices such as metaphors. Technical description relates facts.

Assignments

1. Write a *technical* description of a bookcase with textbooks in it. The description should contain facts, such as measurements, materials, colors, and number and titles of books.

   Example: The brown wooden bookcase held over 300 books, approximate 200 small pocket books, 70 medium size hard-back books, and 50 tall coffee-table books. The five shelves, approximately three feet long, rested in a frame three feet wide by six feet high.

2. Write a *literary* description of a bookcase with textbooks on it. This description should use poetic devices such as personification, metaphor, simile, etc.

   Example: The bookcase groaned under the burden of the heavy, hard-bound books lining its shelves. Creaking like an old man arising from his rocker, the old shelves gave up centuries of knowledge as a borrower lightened its load by removing a volume of Tolstoy's *War and Peace* or Churchill's memoirs.

3. Write two descriptive paragraphs in which you portray one aspect of your home. The first paragraph should be described for an architectural magazine and should be factual. The second paragraph should be for inclusion in a short story and should involve poetic devices as the room develops a personality.

Student Examples

Literary Description

My living room reminds me of a country store that sells American antiques and reproductions. Favorite American phrases appear throughout the room. For example, a large print sings out "God Bless America," while a colorful cross-stitch shouts out "God Bless America." A pewter plaque titled, "The Great American Revolution 1776" shows the surrender of Cornwallis. Even though Christmas comes once a year, a small fake Christmas tree stands decorated with Americana ornaments all year round. Finally, ten different flags of American origin reach out in the various corners of the room. My mother, an American history major, decorated the room in the dominant colors of red, white, and blue.

Technical Description

The aspect of my house that I have chosen to describe is my living room. It's located on the first level on the east side of the house. It is about 22 feet by 14 feet. The carpet is beige with matching beige walls and a blue molding. Two rust-colored armchairs with miniature blue and beige flowers all over them face the large bay window covered with ruffled beige curtains. Another chair that is beige with a rust and blue plaid pattern over it stands next to a matching ottoman where you can rest your feet. Against the longest wall is a six-foot slate-blue couch with two matching pillows on each side. A blue and beige afghan rests on top of the couch. There are a total of five pine tables throughout the room. They hold various lamps, knickknacks, and pictures. Two tall, dark pine bookcases hold seventeen family pictures, one complete set of encyclopedias, and various classical books. Covering the walls are many different American pictures, flags, and cross-stitches. This living room is extremely functional.

The Genres and Subgenres of Workplace English

There are five major genres of workplace literature—correspondence, instructions, reports, proposals, and oral presentations—and a wide variety of minor genres, including templates, feasibility studies, white papers, position papers, newsletters, handouts, minutes to meetings, lab journals, and specifications. Each of these is comprised of a variety of subgenres. For example, correspondence includes letters of application, follow-up letters, and memoranda requesting a service, product, or information.

While we need to provide instruction in the various subgenres, we do not need to teach all of the forms. Most business and technical writing textbooks contain a plethora of documents, but only a small portion of these are written by employees whose jobs fall into the categories we are discussing in this book. Therefore, in this chapter we will discuss only those subgenres in which most employees, regardless of their field or role, communicate.

In teaching these subgenres, we can build on knowledge of the modes of discourse that students acquired when they learned to write the various literary genres. For example, incident reports are written in the narrative mode, observation reports in the descriptive mode, and proposals in the persuasive mode.

The genres and subgenres in this chapter are sequenced according to the frequency with which they are written in the workplace. Notice that those used most frequently are also the ones with which students are most familiar. Thus, I would recommend that templates, correspondence, and instructions be taught in the beginning of an applied English course, and that proposals and reports be taught in the latter part of the course. I would also suggest that while Tech Prep is exclusively a secondary school and community college program, many of these genres can and should be introduced at lower grade levels. All students, regardless of level, can learn to write memoranda to their teachers requesting extended time to complete a project or the opportunity to attend a special assembly, or to propose a topic for a project. Elementary students almost invariably are asked to write reports of field trips. Instead of the traditional chronological description, they can learn to write a focused report that centers around a particular incident or impression, similar to the trip reports employees draft after attending a conference or meeting. Several of the genres, such as proposals and correspondence, easily lend themselves to a student-centered approach.

Templates

Because the use of templates, or forms, has become so pervasive as a means of communicating information in the workplace, we will examine this form first. At one time or another, most of us have filled out an application for a driver's license or a job, reported a car accident or requested vacation or family leave or reimbursement for a conference. Many employees also fill out templates in relation to the people with whom they are in contact, such as clients, customers, and patients, or in relation to incidents in which they are involved, such as accidents.

One profession that relies heavily on notetaking and filling out templates is the Emergency Medical Technician (EMT). These men and women carry pens in their uniform pockets and they record their observations and findings on a glove or a piece of adhesive taped between their knee and ankle while working on the victims at accident sites. Their notes include such medical findings as the victim's pulse rate, blood pressure, and injuries sustained, as well as the actions taken, such as splinting a broken bone or providing CPR. The notes also include their observations of the scene and information from the victims if they are conscious. In the ambulance, EMTs transfer their notes to a field pad. These are used to fill out a hospital form which becomes part of a patient's chart.

Other professions also require employees to fill out templates. Police report each crime they investigate and nurses maintain patients' charts on templates. Manufacturing teams fill out forms identifying each product change they make, and employees witnessing an industrial accident fill out forms describing the incident. Most of these forms serve a double purpose: They provide supervisors and others with up-to-date information on the status of a client or activity, and they also serve as legal documents. If a company is sued because of a product malfunction or a hospital is sued for malpractice, the forms can be used as evidence.

In manufacturing, employees are often required to keep logs, written on templates, in which they record the work done and problems encountered on their shift. The logs are used by employees on the next shift to learn the current status of a line, by supervisors who need to be kept informed about what is being done in their division, and by the employees themselves, who may need to look back on something they did or found during a previous shift. Most templates require employees to fill in blanks and write short responses. Increasingly, templates are being created on-line, with employees entering the data directly from their notes into computers. In fact, many employees who work in the field can now carry notebook computers with them, and enter their information into their institution's data banks from any location.

While templates take care of those items that are common to all respondents in a particular situation, they don't provide for deviations, nor do they provide for extended explanations or descriptions. For example, radiographers' reports may need to indicate that a patient didn't hold his breath while the X rays were taken. For these reasons, most templates include a space for *Comments*. Respondents need to be able to draft descriptions or explanations that relate to one or more aspects of a case in this space, which is usually no more than a third of a page in length.

Implications for the Classroom. To fill out a template accurately and fully, workers need to be aware of the information requested first, so that they can be sure to obtain it while working with a client or patient. They need to take notes that are complete and accurate; they need to be able to interview clients, customers, or patients to obtain all of the information required; and they need to be sharp observers, capable of describing both the small details of an incident as well as the broad context in which an incident occurs. They also need to be able to identify important information, even if it isn't included among the template items, and they need to recognize when situations require additional explanations or descriptions, or when a situation deviates from what is expected.

One method for teaching students to fill in a template is to have them fill out actual forms, such as a passport application. The application can be obtained from your local post office. You can also have them work in pairs, with one member assuming the role of the postal clerk, the other the applicant. The postal clerk can interview the applicant and then fill out the passport form. Students can switch roles so each has an opportunity to fill out an application for the other. The Regional Airport Authority of Louisville and Jefferson County, Missouri, developed the following activities related to international travel, something in which many students may eventually need to engage if they work for an international company.

LESSON:	TRAVEL ABROAD
TIME FRAME:	5 lessons
GOALS:	Researching Listening Writing
OUTCOMES:	Students will demonstrate the ability to complete an application. Students will determine where to find information related to their lives. Students will determine where to find information related to international travel laws.
MATERIALS:	Passport application
PROCEDURE:	1. Discuss the differences between traveling from state to state and country to country. 2. Explain that a person needs a passport to visit another country. Discuss where you get a passport application (federal buildings and post offices). 3. Have students fill out a passport application.
EXTENSION:	1. Have students research what other requirements they might have when visiting a foreign country, e.g., a visa, proof of vaccination, etc. Have them research why these laws exist. 2. Have students select a country and then create a brochure for potential tourists. The brochure should include information on requirements for visiting that country.

To carry out this activity successfully, students need to receive instruction in the following:

- note taking
- interviewing
- differentiating between relevant and unnecessary information
- using appropriate technical abbreviations
- writing truncated sentences in appropriate text grammars
- researching information over the Internet, by telephone, or in personal interviews to discover how to obtain a birth certificate and to find out about international travel laws
- writing letters of request for birth certificates and for information on international travel laws

To prepare students to fill out templates appropriately, completely, and accurately, students need practice in the following:

- filling out forms accurately and completely on paper and computer
- writing brief paragraphs describing deviations from expected conditions on paper and on computer
- writing brief paragraphs expanding on information provided in template form on paper and on computer

Correspondence

Correspondence includes four subgenres: letters, memoranda, electronic mail, and facsimiles. Students need to know the standard formats and conventions for each, and how each is used.

Correspondence is written for a variety of purposes: to inform, to make a request, to respond to a request, to introduce an attached document such as a proposal or report, to provide negative news, to follow up an interview, to apply for a job, to report on a meeting, to sell a product or service, or to order a product or service.

Correspondence can serve in two capacities: It can contain a document within it, or it can introduce a separate attached document. For example, an employee may be expected to submit a report to the Chief Financial Officer (CFO) that presents the results of a survey to determine the number of workers interested in using an on-site day care facility. The employee may be able to present this information in a one- or two-page memorandum. On the other hand, the employee may find that the information is sufficiently complex to require a long report. In this case, she will probably draft it as an independent document, and send it with a cover memo that tells readers why they are receiving an attached report.

Much of the correspondence written by workers relates to the day-to-day management of their institutions, and to the routine tasks for which they are responsible; they seldom have communication with people outside their corporations. Because much of the day-to-day business is communicated among the employees themselves, and between the employees and their supervisors, the majority of their correspondence is in the form of memoranda rather than letters, and is often transmitted via E-mail. These memoranda are usually concerned with such routine information as the time, date, and place of the next team meeting, the latest method for recycling office waste, or with such conventional needs as a request for the latest updates on a software program or a request for additional information about a patient. Because the majority of the correspondence in which employees engage is in the form of a memorandum, we will concentrate on that subgenre.

Readers don't often have the time to read a memo as soon as it reaches their desk or appears in their electronic mail. However, the message may be of immediate concern. Because readers need to know whether or not they should look at a memo immediately, the subject line is extremely important. If the subject line in the memo discussed in Figure 3–2 had read "Repair of Freight Tunnel to Prevent Flooding of Financial District and Million Dollar Mile," instead of the more innocuous "Freight Tunnel Repair," the 1992 Chicago flood might have been prevented.

On Monday, April 13, 1992, downtown Chicago came to a standstill. Freight tunnels that had been dug underneath the city in the early part of the century were being flooded by the Chicago river. Water was seeping into the basements of office buildings in the city's financial district, and into its retail area where department stores, such as Marshall Field's, are located. All buildings in the area were evacuated and traffic halted. It took the city weeks to pump all the water out. The cost in closed businesses and ruined inventory ran in the billions.

The cause of the flood was a leak in the wall of the tunnel abutting the river. Several weeks earlier Louis Koncza, the chief engineer for the Bureau of Bridges in the city's Department of Transportation (DOT), had sent the memo to John LaPlante, DOT Commissioner, notifying him of the leak and requesting permission to repair the walls. Why wasn't the wall repaired before the leak became a flood?

One of the reasons was the failure of the reader to recognize the significance of the problem. If the subject line had focused on the effect

Figure 3–2

TO: John M. LaPlante
FROM: Louis Koncza
SUBJECT: Freight Tunnel Repair

On March 13, 1992, city forces discovered a damaged section of concrete wall in the freight tunnel which passes under the North Branch of the Chicago River along Kinzie Street. The damaged wall area is approximately 20 feet long by 6 feet high. Some soil from beneath the river has flowed into the tunnel and this flow is slowly continuing.

Investigation into the cause of the damage reveals that on September 30, 1991, new pile clusters were installed under a city contract to replace old deteriorated piles. . . . It appears that the added lateral soil pressure exerted by the new piles resulted in wall failure of the freight tunnel which is very close to the pile cluster.

This wall failure should be repaired immediately due to the potential danger of flooding out the entire freight tunnel system which is quite extensive. The City is currently receiving revenue by renting sections of the tunnel system to cable and fiber optic companies.

The most expedient and economic solution to this problem is to install foot thick brick masonry bulkheads . . .

The estimated cost of repair is approximately $10,000.00 and it will take City crews approximately two weeks to construct the bulkheads.

With your approval, work will begin as soon as possible.

---

of the problem—the flooding of an extremely important part of the city—rather than on the cause, the reader might have placed a higher priority on the job.

Readers also need to know what they are expected to do with a memo—whether they need to act on the information, respond to a request, use the information to make a decision, or pass the information on to someone else. An explanation of the purpose for a memorandum should be placed at the very beginning, so the reader is mentally prepared not only to accept the message but to use it appropriately. Luckily, LaPlante read the entire memo. Otherwise he would never have known it was a request for his approval to have the leak repaired, since the writer doesn't ask for approval until the final paragraph.

Implications for the Classroom. There are many opportunities to make authentic assignments in which students are required to write a memorandum. I often ask them to write a memo to me when they want to know something, for example, when a report is due, how long it should be, whether they can use the computer lab or library. I respond either on the memo or with a separate memo in the same way that responses are made in the workplace.

The Manitoba Board of Education and Training recommends the assignment, instructional materials, and model in Figure 3–3 to provide students with experience in drafting a letter, since employees occasionally need to write to people outside their organizations.

To enable students to correspond in writing, they need to receive instruction in the following:

- conventions for letters, memoranda, E-mail, fax
- standard formats for letters, memoranda, E-mail, fax
- writing concise, specific, and accurate subject lines
- writing an introductory paragraph that explains the purpose of a piece of correspondence
- sequencing information from most to least important
- writing concisely
- maintaining a friendly and positive tone
- writing persuasively

To prepare students to write effective memoranda, they need practice writing the following:

- memoranda that provide information
- memoranda that request information
- memoranda that respond to requests
- memoranda that serve as cover correspondence

Communication Related to Acquiring a Job

Among the most important forms of communication that students need to know if they are to enter the workforce are those associated with acquiring a job. These include letters of application, resumes, follow-up letters, telephone requests for an interview, responses to interview requests, and interviews. While many job openings are still announced in newspapers, an increasing number of companies advertise jobs on the Internet and encourage applicants to send their letters of application and resumes over the Internet.

It takes about twenty seconds for human resource personnel reading letters of application to make up their minds whether an applicant qualifies for a position. Thus, the initial appearance of a letter and the

Figure 3–3

Assignment: A Problem with the Company's VCR

You are a technician working for Marsden Manufacturing. Two years ago the company authorized you to buy a VCR and TV for showing training videos to the manufacturing staff. You bought them from the local branch of Multiple Sales Company (MSC) and paid $389.50 for the VCR and $575 for the TV. The VCR was a Nabuchi model 202, and the TV was a Sharpe model 1800. The purchase was made on MSC's sales slip No. 4726.

Two months ago—on January 6—the VCR failed and you took it to MSC for repair. The local manager (Jim Warbush) wrote up Work Order M1831 and gave you a copy.

You phoned Jim Warbush every few days and he kept saying he was waiting for parts. Finally, after seven weeks—on February 24—he admitted he couldn't fix the VCR. You picked it up the same day and took it to Phoenix TV Repair for a second opinion. Within 24 hours Wes Phoenix told you the VCR was beyond repair and handed you Work Order 1304 on which one of his technicians had written: "Previous repair shop reassembled the unit with the power supply put in backwards, blew almost every component."

You bought a replacement VCR from Phoenix for $380.

When you told Jim Warbush at MSC what you had found out, he admitted his technician had destroyed the VCR. You asked for a cash settlement of half the value of the new VCR (=$190). He agreed that that was reasonable, but now, three weeks later you are still waiting for a cheque.

Write to Wanda Shewchuk, the Customer Service Manager at Multiple Sales Company's head office in Toronto. Describe the problem and ask for reimbursement. The address is 2720 Claremont Boulevard, Toronto, ON, M5W1X8

Instructional Material

A complaint letter expects the reader to take corrective action:

(continued)

Figure 3–3 (*continued*)

In the following letter to a credit card company, the four writing compartments are clearly defined.

Dear Customer Accounts Manager:

Summary Statement
There is an error on my October 5 WorldCard statement that has resulted in an overcharge which I am asking you to correct.

Background
My WorldCard Account number is 312465897, the entry is item 4 dated September 9, the vendor is Burntwood Auto Service, the control number is 0147162, and the dollar entry is $272.40.

Complaint Details
My records for this item show that I bought 51.02 litres of gasoline at 53.4 cents per litre, which calculates out as $27.24. This is exactly one-tenth of the amount shown on my statement, which indicates that a decimal point error has occurred.

Action Statement
Please credit my account with $245.16, which is the difference between $27.24 and $272.40, and reverse any interest charges that have been applied.

Model

MARSDEN MANUFACTURING

Wanda Shewchuk
Customer Service Manager
Multiple Sales Company
2720 Claremont Boulevard
Toronto, ON
M5W 1X8

Dear Ms. Shewchuk:

We have received unsatisfactory service from your Winnipeg Branch and I am appealing to you to resolve the problem.

The incident concerns a Nabuchi model 202 VCR, which we purchased from your Winnipeg Branch in March 1992 on MSC's sales slip No. 4726.

(*continued*)

Figure 3–3 (*continued*)

On January 6, 1994 I took the VCR to your Winnipeg office for repair. After seven weeks Mr. Jim Warbush, your Winnipeg office manager, informed me that the VCR could not be repaired. I then took it to Phoenix TV Repair for a second opinion. They discovered that when MSC reassembled the VCR they installed the power supply backwards, which blew almost every component in the VCR (see attached copy of Phoenix TV Repair's work order).

We have had to purchase a new VCR, and have suggested to Mr. Warbush that MSC in Winnipeg should bear half the purchase cost, which would be $190. He agreed, but has made no attempt to pay us. I am asking you either to instruct Mr. Warbush to originate a cheque, or for MSC in Toronto to send the cheque to us (payable to Marsden Manufacturing).

Sincerely,

In this letter: Para 1 is the **Summary Statement**
Para 2 contains the **Background Information**
Para 3 contains the **Complaint Details**
Para 4 is the **Action Statement**

first paragraph are crucial. Omitting the name of the company or the position for which the applicant is applying in the first paragraph, or failing to correct a spelling or usage error may result in a flat rejection, regardless of the individual's qualifications.

After a letter of application and resume are sent, an applicant may initiate a telephone call to request an interview or, if the company is interested in the applicant, a representative from the Human Resources division may call the applicant to schedule a meeting. Human resource personnel use these telephone conversations to evaluate the ability of applicants to communicate verbally as well as their resourcefulness, patience, and ability to deal with frustration if they are unable to get through to the person they are calling. Such conversations always need to be conducted in a sociable and pleasant but formal tone.

Human resource personnel are also interested in employees' social skills. They are impressed with follow-up letters after an interview that thank the company for its time.

The interview, in essence, is the final performance. The company is looking for people who dress appropriately, are knowledgeable and enthusiastic about the company and its products, and can verbalize their own strengths in relation to the position they are seeking.

Implications for the Classroom. I often have students write a letter of application and a resume for a job in which they might be interested after they graduate. As a follow-up, I have found that human resource personnel in local industries may be willing to visit a classroom to hold mock interviews with students to initiate them into the process.

Sharon Strenth, an English teacher at Kouts High School in Indiana, has students write a thank-you note for a useless gift as a prewriting lesson to learn to draft thank-you letters for business.

Students select a silly or ugly gift that they have received. Then Sharon helps them analyze their audience and their purpose for writing a thank-you note for the gift. Students enjoy this aspect of the activity, often describing Aunt Rosa's eccentricities or Uncle Joe's bad taste in ties. Next Sharon instructs the class on the conventions of a thank-you letter. Students then draft, peer edit, and revise their notes. Finally, they post them on the class bulletin board so everyone can read them. Following this lesson, it is not difficult for Sharon to move students to the next step, writing a formal thank you letter, which she includes as part of her unit on communicating to get a job.

If students are to learn to gather information related to job openings and then apply successfully for a job, they need to receive instruction in the following:

- locating and reading job openings in newspapers and on the Internet
- conventions for letters of application, resumes, and follow-up letters
- standard formats for letters of application, resumes, and follow-up letters
- conventions for E-mailing letters of application and resumes
- determining appropriate information for inclusion in a letter of application
- determining appropriate information for inclusion in a resume
- transmission of letters of application and resumes over the Internet
- proofreading skills
- peer editing techniques

had an opportunity to introduce most of the major concepts of the course, while providing a framework in which to teach the other genres. The completed handbook, the work of two classes, was given to the library.

The following set of instructions was one of several I received.

DIRECTIONS FOR PLAYING HACKEY-SACK

Definition
A Hackey-Sack is a small leather sack filled with beans.

Object
Hackey-Sack is a game of skill in which there are neither winners nor losers. The object is to keep the Hackey-Sack in the air, using only your feet to do so.

Equipment
One (1) Hackey-Sack

Number of Players
1–6 players

Rules
1. Use only your feet
2. Don't hog the ball
3. Don't push or shove

Directions
The game is played differently, depending on the number of players.

One player
Toss the sack lightly in the air, using your feet to keep it in the air as long as possible.

Two players
1. Stand about five feet away and face the other player. Begin with a coin toss. The person winning the toss plays first.
2. Toss the sack lightly in the air. Use your feet to keep it in the air as long as possible. When the sack falls to the ground, it is the second person's turn.

Three to six players

1. Make a circle with a space of about two feet between each player. Face the center of the circle.
2. Select someone to start. Try to keep the sack in the air either by using your own feet or by kicking the sack to someone else in the circle.

   When the sack touches the ground, the round ends and a new round begins. A different player begins the round.

To write in this genre, students need to receive instruction in the following:

- the text grammars for instructions and procedures
- the standard formats for instructions, documentation, and procedures
- the conventions of instructions, documentation, and procedures
- visual text and its use in instructions
- graphics and their use in instructions
- writing in modules
- collaboration in writing a manual
- testing to determine the usability of the instructions

To help students write successfully, they need practice in the following:

- writing instructions
- task-oriented, job-specific software documentation
- job procedures

Proposals

Proposals are written for three purposes: to request permission to make a change in the workplace; to request support for working on a project; and to offer to provide a product or service. Most employees will have opportunities to write proposals relating to changes in the workplace; only a few will have opportunities to work on the other types of proposals. American Electric and Power (AEP) is one of many companies that not only encourage workers to propose changes to improve the workplace, but provide monetary incentives ranging from $25 to $1,000. At the Central Illinois Light Company, the bonus is a percentage of the money saved, which can go as high as $10,000. Employees who submit accepted proposals may find themselves promoted and given more responsibility as their supervisors recognize their problem-solving capabilities.

Implications for the Classroom. Proposals provide an opportunity for instruction in one of the major traditional modes of discourse—persuasion. In writing a proposal, the writer needs to convince the reader to approve the changes being suggested.

This genre also offers an opportunity to teach some of the major skills required for engaging in academic writing, especially in gathering, citing, and referencing sources. To document a problem and develop valid arguments for a solution, employees may need to refer to a variety of sources to support their viewpoints. Unlike the academic research paper, which relies heavily on books and professional journals by authorities in the field, the sources for a workplace proposal may include such documents as brochures, advertisements, company newsletters, and specification sheets. Often this information can be located on the Internet. Field sources, such as interviews and observations of situations, may also be used. These need to be cited in the text and listed as references at the end of a proposal.

Instead of the author/page style for citations, which is based on MLA guidelines, the author/year style should be used for the applied sciences, and the numerical style for the theoretical sciences. There are many reference books available which contain the guidelines for these styles.

Proposals also offer opportunities to provide instruction in several organizational patterns. A proposal follows a problem/solution pattern. The writer describes a problem and then explains its solution. The problem section usually follows a cause/effect pattern in reverse order. The writer describes a problem (the effect of a situation) and then explains the cause. The solution has several subsections, including a section listing the advantages gained by adopting the proposed solution, and a budget section comparing the cost of the proposed solution with the present cost. Graphics, in the form of schematics, diagrams, and photographs, are often included with proposals.

Proposals provide an almost infinite set of possibilities for engaging students in student-centered activities. There are always situations in a school, community, or home that can be improved. Your school

may need to find new ways to raise funds to upgrade computers, purchase additional software, institute a recycling program, or solve a
parking problem.

Students can be assigned to write a proposal suggesting solutions
to problems such as these. This approach requires considerable prewriting instruction. Students need to learn skills in team management, consensus building and problem solving, interviewing and
observation techniques, writing trip reports, designing questions for
and analyzing responses to interviews and surveys, and gathering and
citing sources.

You may want to assign a project, or you may be willing to give
your students autonomy to make the decision. The latter approach
provides an opportunity to teach consensus building. To decide on a
problem and on a solution to that problem, students will need to
arrive at a consensus. They'll also need to formulate a plan for per-
suading their reader(s) that a problem exists and that their solution is
a viable one. In relation to this task, they will have to find written
information about the topic as well as conduct interviews and observe
similar situations to gather field data.

Ron Blicq developed the activity in Figure 3–4 for the Manitoba
Department of Education to teach proposal writing. To engage in the
various activities leading to the writing of a proposal, students need to
receive instruction in the following:

- the conventions for writing proposals to make a change
- the standard format for writing proposals to make a change
- gathering and using appropriate sources to support arguments
- citing sources
- computing costs
- developing a budget
- explaining a budget
- writing about numbers
- comparing/contrasting items and sums
- writing persuasive discourse
- describing a problem
- explaining a solution to a problem
- developing a problem/solution organizational pattern
- developing a cause/effect organizational pattern
- using schematics, diagrams, or photographs to illustrate an object
  or a process

Figure 3–4

Improving Traffic Flow and Student Parking at the High School:
Sample Umbrella Project

Rationale   Many students drive cars to school, but there is
                         rarely enough parking. Additionally, some students
                         are driven to school, creating an access problem for
                         staff and drivers. Either or both of these situations
                         can be evaluated.

Suggested Method   The class is told they are to investigate the problem
                     and develop a proposal for its resolution. The
                     proposal will intitially be targeted to the school
                     principal, but the secondary readers will be the
                     school division, which will approve the
                     expenditure of funds.

The project will require students to:
- survey the staff and students to identify the extent of the problem and the number of parking stalls students need
- identify a suitable area of the school property that could be assigned to student parking (or, if no school property is available, a nearby vacant lot that might be used)
- determine if there are zoning restrictions or other constraints that might inhibit developing the area into a parking lot
- design the parking area for optimum use
- determine how stalls are to be separated (i.e., solely by lines on the asphalt, or by fences between rows
- decide whether power is to be supplied, for cars to plug in
- determine the cost
- evaluate the feasibility of running the parking lot on a cost recovery basis, which embraces
  1. identifying who would administer the parking lot and collect fees
  2. considering bonding of the person or group who does this
  3. determining where the *front end* money is to come from

(continued)

Figure 3–4 (*continued*)

- decide how the parking lots are to be allocated (presumably, by a democratic process) because inevitably there will be insufficient lots to satisfy all the students

Some of the activities that evolve from this scenario are:

1. breaking the class into project groups, each to address a different aspect
2. devising a survey form and a method for administering it to the staff and whole student body
3. writing letters to various organizations to determine that
   - the school administration (e.g., principal) is aware of (and approves of) the project
   - space is available (or nearby land can be rented)
   - no city bylaws will inhibit the plan
   - if an entry and exit are to be built, no traffic laws will be violated
4. writing letters asking for cost estimates
5. writing progress reports
6. describing (orally) the results of each group's research to the rest of the class
7. holding meetings, as a class and within each group, to discuss progress
8. establishing a project plan, target activity dates, and deadlines
9. writing a proposal to present to the school administration
10. presenting the proposal orally to the school administration

Some other learning experiences that may evolve from the projects are:

- managing a project
- working as a team
- writing collaboratively
- dealing with bureaucracy—by telephone, by letter, face-to-face

To enable students to write proposals that are accepted by their readers, they need practice in the following:

- writing proposals to make a change using a template
- writing proposals to make a change using free form
- computing project costs
- developing budgets
- comparing costs
- writing persuasive discourse

Reports

Reports are composed of numerous subgenres. The ones our students will probably encounter on their jobs include progress, periodic, and activity reports; information, observation, and incident reports; and recommendation and evaluation reports. Most of these reports will be written for supervisors who need to keep up with what is happening in their divisions. Often supervisors synthesize the reports from individual employees in a division to create a division report that they send to *their* supervisors.

Progress, Activity, and Periodic Reports. Progress and activity reports are usually written by employees involved in projects that can range from the installation of a new production line to the inception of cross training within a bank division, to the initiation of a new schedule for meeting accounts payable, to the establishment of a team to consider improving diversity in the workplace. Progress and activity reports are usually composed of three sections: work to date that's been completed on a project; present status of a project; and future plans for completing a project. A fourth section, *concerns,* is sometimes included.

Periodic reports may be written daily, weekly, monthly, or annually, to document work that has been done during a specific segment of time. The report allows supervisors to determine whether production/services are up or down, whether problems exist, and if previous problems have been solved. The reports provide managers with data to see trends in their divisions. These reports may follow an analytic organizational pattern, and be divided according to the various activities in which an employee has engaged during a specific period, or they may follow a chronological organizational pattern in which the discussion is divided according to specific periods of time.

Information, Observation, and Incident Reports. Employees usually write these reports as the result of a request by their supervisor.
For example, dieticians provide patients with nutrition information to
use when they are released from a hospital; police officers report what
they did and saw at the scene of a crime or when they arrested a sus-
pect; and assembly line workers report what they saw if they were
present when an accident occurred.

Information reports usually follow an analytic pattern, in which
the text is organized around the various chunks of information that
are included. Incident and observation reports follow a chronological pattern, presenting the activities or observations relating to the
main incident or subject under observation as they occurred in real
time.

Evaluation and Recommendation Reports. Traditionally, workers were evaluated by those above them. Today, however, workers
have an opportunity to evaluate those above them as well as to evaluate each other. Furthermore, supervisors can no longer peremptorily
decide a worker's merits. Instead, supervisors are expected to collaborate with their employees in an evaluation. Thus, employees are now
responsible for writing evaluations relating to themselves, their peers,
and their supervisors. In addition, with the inception of TQM, divisions are responsible for evaluating themselves. Thus, both as individuals and as members of a team, workers are expected to write
evaluations of their jobs in relation to meeting their company's goals.

The utility company, Cilco, asks employees to consider such
questions as "Is the process I use to do my job or achieve my goals
too cumbersome or outdated?" and "Are there functions that I perform that are redundant or outmoded?" It is implied that if the
answers to questions such as these are in the affirmative, employees
will suggest changes to improve the conditions. Thus, all evaluations
are expected to indicate opportunities for improvement. For example, recommendations related to the questions above might include a
request to acquire new technology for making a job more efficient
and effective.

Evaluation and recommendation reports usually begin with a
background or overview section that includes an explanation of the
report's purpose. The report then includes a section listing the results
of the evaluation, and a section listing the recommendations. If
employees are asked to look at a project, a production line, or a situation or incident, then a section that explains how the evaluation was
conducted and the criteria used for evaluating it should be inserted
after the background section.

Reports often include a variety of ancillary documents, including transmittal correspondence, a title page, an executive summary, table of contents, glossary, and appendix. The ones these employees will write will probably include only a cover memo, title page, and appendix, or the report may be sufficiently short to be written as a memorandum. These reports may also involve the use of graphics and visual text.

Implications for the Classroom

Whenever my students are working on a major project, I have them draft a progress report in the form of a memo. Not only does it give them practice in this subgenre, but it gives me an opportunity to identify those students who are falling behind schedule or having problems.

I often tie final reports to projects students are doing for other courses. When I can't do this, I create an activity for which students will write a report. Information, observation, and incident reports can be tied in with lessons on templates because they serve as the narration sections of a template.

Evaluation and recommendation reports reports fit naturally into a student-centered classroom. At the end of a project I request that students write an evaluation report of the project and of each of their team members, so that I can take each student's participation in teamwork into consideration when I determine a grade. The students and I decide jointly on the list of criteria to be used in these evaluations.

I find that creating scenarios and assigning roles to students is a good method for teaching students to write recommendation reports. Mary Yorke, an English teacher at Munster High School in Indiana, developed the following problem-solving activity which requires students to write a recommendation report.

Problem-Based Learning Lesson

Approach

- Use real-life situations to heighten interest in a topic.
- Discuss metacognitive techniques.
- Encourage students to work cooperatively.
- Foster listening skills.

- Teach the importance of audience when writing.
- Teach the proper use of interviewing techniques.
- Employ coaching techniques to enhance teaching skills.

Objectives

- Students will learn how to weigh the value of material used in sound expository writing.
- Students will generate ideas about where to find support material for their writing.
- Students will share with their peers the material they gather.
- Students will discern between worthwhile and worthless information.
- Students will interview people currently involved in their problem.
- Students will learn how to think so that they can become lifelong problem solvers.
- Students will learn the complexity of issues that they must write about.

Activity

1. The teacher will provide the students with a loosely woven problem.
2. As a group, the students will identify what is known about the problem, what is unknown, and where to turn for answers.
3. The students will listen to one another's reasoning to determine how other individuals deal with complex problems.
4. Students will gather materials and write a concise explanation of the information that they feel will help deal with the problem.
5. Students will share the information gathered.
6. Students will learn to search again when gaps are discovered in information.
7. Students will write a major paper weighing all the information provided by the entire class.

The Situation

You are the principal of Munster High School, and the school board is considering whether they should eliminate tracking in the high school's English classes. The school board has asked you to make a recommendation on the future of tracking in the high school's English classes. Your report is due at the next school board meeting, which is Tuesday, September 5.

The problem as I see it: How to make an informed decision about whether to retain tracking or not.

Possible Sources: students

teachers

parents

administrators

library research

other schools in the area

lawyers

Shelagh Gallagher

Metacognitive Skills: intellectual curiosity

intellectual discipline

intellectual responsibility

Enduring Concept: Numerous systems affect a decision.

Tracking

Legal aspects

state laws

size inequality

teacher attention

projects that are more engaging and challenging

college entrance advantages

Academic aspects

locked into track

gifted and talented programs

grade inflation

college prep

materials used

AP tests
teaching strategies
how students are tracked

Economic aspects

students per teacher
materials
number of classrooms
number of staff members

Social aspects

elitism
leadership
labels
image and esteem
competitiveness/defeatism
rights and privileges
town environment

Basis for tracking

educational theory
political correctness
arbitrary decisions

To acquire skills and strategies required for writing effective reports, students need to receive instruction in the following:

- the conventions for writing each type of report
- the standard format for each type of report
- organizing chunks of related information
- developing a chronology of events
- writing a chronological narration
- observing details and overall context of an incident
- describing a situation factually

- evaluating performance in relation to stated goals
- reading budgets
- calculating costs
- comparing costs to budgets
- organizing information in the following patterns:
  - analytical pattern
  - chronological pattern
- conducting a self-evaluation
- evaluating peers
- evaluating supervisors
- evaluating work performance of individuals, teams, and divisions in relation to company goals
- collaborating with a supervisor on a self-evaluation
- developing recommendations based on results of evaluations
- writing cover memos
- developing a title page
- determining the information that belongs in an appendix and creating an appendix
- using appropriate graphics
- using visual text appropriately

To write the various types of reports, students need practice in the following:

- writing progress, activity, and periodic reports
- writing information, observation, and incident reports
- writing evaluation and recommendation reports
- collaborating on a self-evaluation
- evaluating people, divisions, and job performance
- reading budgets

Oral Presentations

The introduction of teamwork into the workplace has provided workers with an excellent opportunity for having a voice. However, unless employees express their concerns and suggest their ideas, they remain disenfranchised. Voicing one's ideas in a group discussion is a form of oral presentation, and employees need to acquire skills for participating actively in team meetings as well as learning skills for making short oral presentations at these meetings.

Many employees are members of committees that are composed of representatives from a variety of divisions, not just their own. Members may not only be expected to present their division's ideas to the committee, but they may also be expected to present the committee's ideas to their division.

Many of these presentations can be made more effective with the use of visuals, including overhead transparencies and slides. Often these are made with fairly simple software programs. Recently posters have gained popularity. Handouts can also be distributed at these presentations, to provide listeners with additional information that can be read later when there is time.

Implications for the Classroom

I usually integrate oral presentations with other types of communication, such as proposal or report writing. However, because presenting ideas and responding to ideas in team meetings is as important as making formal presentations, I try to be aware of students who are not participating in class discussions, and to help them acquire skills for this type of oral communication. Because students are more willing to participate if they have time to consider what they will say, I often require students, either as homework or as a five-minute in-class assignment, to write down their ideas or responses prior to a class discussion.

Students need to receive instruction in the following:

- drafting short, three-minute presentations to propose an idea
- drafting short, three-minute presentations to inform listeners about a new program, strategy, or procedure
- drafting short, three-minute presentations to persuade listeners to agree to a new strategy, program, or procedure
- making short, three-minute presentations
- creating visuals to accompany presentations in the form of slides, transparencies, and posters
- developing handouts to accompany presentations

Students need opportunities to practice the following:

- making three-minute presentations with accompanying handouts and visuals to propose an idea, inform listeners about a new program, strategy, or procedure, or persuade listeners to agree to a new program, strategy, or procedure

Telephone and Voice Mail

Teenagers' use of the telephone is legendary. Yet, students' knowledge of telephone etiquette is slight, and many become tongue-tied when confronted with the need to leave a message on a recorder or on voice mail. Students need to learn appropriate telephone etiquette because, despite the impact of electronic mail, the telephone—with its various auxiliaries, such as voice mail—is a major source of business communication.

Employees' relationships with clients or customers over a telephone can influence their listeners' decisions to purchase products or services. Thus, it is essential that students learn to use appropriate telephone etiquette in their communication with those outside their company, and that they learn to listen carefully in order to relay messages or place correct orders.

Voice mail is a new addition to telephone communication, and all too often people feel intimidated by it because they are unsure of what they should say, either in recording a message on their own phone line, or in leaving a message for the person they have called. They need to learn to create appropriate messages so callers know whether to leave a message and whether the person will return soon. They also need to learn to respond to a voice mail message by either leaving a request for a return call, or stating the information they want to communicate.

Implications for the Classroom

A wide variety of scenarios can be developed, in which students team up to practice telephone etiquette as they assume the role of either the caller or the receiver.

Students need to receive instruction in the following:

- the conventions of telephone etiquette
- the conventions of voice mail etiquette
- answering a telephone for themselves
- answering a telephone for someone else
- speaking on a telephone
- drafting a message for their own voice mail
- drafting a message to respond to someone's voice mail
- providing information, responding to requests, making requests

Students need practice in the following:

- holding a telephone conversation when they place a call
- holding a telephone conversation whey then receive a call

- holding a telephone conversation when they receive a call for someone else
- recording a message on their recorder or voice mail
- leaving a message on someone's recorder or voice mail

Miscellaneous

Some employees may be engaged in other forms of communication, including proposals to offer a product or service, white papers and position papers, feasibility studies, electronic mail, newsletters and announcements, posters, general public communications, minutes to meetings, lab journals, and specifications.

Proposals to Offer a Product or Service. This type of proposal, which is similar to an advertisement, is usually written by people who are self-employed. People in technological fields, who develop a product or perform technical operations, and people in the health sciences and criminal justice areas, who offer their particular services independently of a company, may send these proposals to potential customers to persuade them to order a product or contract for a service. The document is usually in the form of a letter.

White Papers and Position Papers. These are advanced report forms which are usually written by managers or professional personnel at the request of a supervisor or administrator. The purpose of a white paper, which bears a close resemblance to an academic research paper, is to provide an administrator with as much information as possible about a topic so that the reader can use the information to make a decision. For example, a vice president of marketing for a paper company may want to know about landfills in southern cities with a population of approximately 100,000. The vice president needs the information to determine whether or not to market a new type of trash bag that disintegrates quickly in temperatures above 75 degrees Fahrenheit.

A position paper is similar to a white paper. However, in this subgenre, the writer assumes a position in relation to the information. For example, the same vice president may ask the writer to provide a position paper on whether or not middle-size southern cities are sufficiently concerned about landfill space that they would recommend citizens purchase the company's bags.

Feasibility Studies. These studies are usually conducted to determine whether or not a proposed project is feasible. The organization of the study is very similar to recommendation and evaluation reports. The report usually examines several alternatives and suggests the pros and cons of each. It may or may not recommend one of the alternatives above the others.

Electronic Mail. Electronic mail (E-mail) is used by many businesses to transmit routine messages. It is less formal than hard-copy memoranda. Often sentences are truncated, and abbreviations and acronyms abound. However, the message must still be literate and understood by the receiver. Writers must be careful that sentences contain the major speech parts in appropriate order, and that abbreviations and acronyms that readers may not know are explained. E-mail has its own set of conventions, which need to be followed.

Newsletters and Announcements. As companies empower employees to manage their own workplace environment, it has become increasingly important for employees to be kept informed of what is occurring in their company. One form in which this information is communicated is through a newsletter. While some of the information for a newsletter still comes from management, a great deal must now come from the employees themselves. Thus, an increasing number of workers are becoming involved in writing articles for newsletters, which follow the basic conventions of journalistic news and feature writing. Guidelines for writing these documents can be found in any basic journalism textbook.

Because various teams, especially those that cross divisions, are often responsible for developing programs, events, and even social activities, employees are also involved in writing announcements. The availability of software programs for word processing and desktop publishing have made these tasks both enjoyable and creative enterprises for those employees who have skills in these two programs.

Posters. Posters have become a popular form of communication over the past few years. They can often be seen at conferences of technical and health professionals. While at most conferences only authorities with national reputations in a field are invited to speak, many attendees have conducted interesting research or developed a unique concept. Posters allow these people to present their ideas or products. The presentation is usually made in an informal session in which participants wander about a room, looking at and reading those posters that catch their attention. The speakers, standing by their posters, can talk to the onlookers for a few moments about their topic and respond to questions. The number of posters included in a session may range from five to twenty-five. The object of a poster is to present the major points of a topic and accompanying visuals. Posters are usually viewed by two to ten people at a time, from a distance of two to seven feet. Therefore, the visuals and text need to be large. The designer of a poster should be sure to follow the rubrics for visuals, graphics, and layout design.

Posters are also being adopted as a visual aid for presentations, especially of proposals, to small groups, ranging from three to twenty individuals. The advantage of a poster during a small presentation is that it can be left with those in attendance for further study.

Communication for the General Public. Employees are seldom asked to write for the general public, which has no knowledge of their field. However, occasionally, workers are asked by a church or community group, their child's school, or an organization to which their spouse belongs to discuss some aspect of their work. Often these requests are for oral presentations.

Occasionally, too, workers may be asked to write a description of a project on which they are working for inclusion in a newsletter that goes to the company's clients or customers who are probably not familiar with the technical aspects of the field. If the company is large, a member of the public relations staff reviews and edits the description before it is released. However, in a small company the description may be released directly.

Minutes to Meetings. Minutes are short documents reporting on the actions taken at a meeting. Employees who work for a company that is using teamwork may find themselves attending a number of meetings every month. A record, reporting the discussions and decisions made at these meetings, needs to be kept and distributed to the members. Because many of the meetings involve issues and decisions related to the company, the work environment, and job procedures, the minutes are important documents that provide managers with information on new rules, regulations, and procedures. Minutes also serve as historical and legal documents to which people can refer in determining the intent of a particular decision. Many employees in team-oriented jobs find themselves at one time or another responsible for taking notes at a meeting and then writing them up as minutes. The conventions and form for minutes can be found in *Robert's Rules of Order* (Robert [1876] 1990).

Lab Journals. Experiments requiring lab journals are not limited to research and development units of a large company. Today, many areas of a company are engaged in experiments to determine better, cost efficient, and safer processes and products. For example, an area in Caterpillar's engine division is working on innovative paint-dipping procedures for engines. Although the research and development division came up with the new procedure, the paint division is responsible for field testing and improving the procedure so that it is effective in actual practice, not just in theory.

When employees engage in an experiment, such as the one involving paint-dipping procedures, they keep a daily journal to provide a permanent record of their day-to-day work. Once they've completed the experiment, they use their journal records to write a report synthesizing the work they've done. These journals not only serve as information reports so that employees' supervisors know what they have done, but as historical and legal documents that can be researched in the future to learn how a procedure was developed. The conventions and format for a lab journal can be found in many scientific and technical textbooks.

Specifications. Specifications are among the most important forms of writing in which people employed in technological fields engage. A specification describes a particular product or process, so that it can be bought, produced, developed, or built "by others to the complete satisfaction of all concerned" (Ayers 1975, 2). If the appropriate amount of concrete for an upper floor is not specified properly, the floor could crack or, worse, break. Specifications are legal documents that: inform owners as to what to expect from a contractor, provide the basis of estimated costs in bidding a job, define work for contractors, establish the quality and quantity of materials in a product, provide instruction in the installation of materials, and establish a standard by which a product or process can be evaluated.

Implications for the Classroom

In a student-centered classroom, the opportunity to introduce these subgenres occurs often. If a class decides to raise money for an activity, students can write a product or service proposal. If students have access to Internet, they can correspond with students at another school via E-mail. Using desktop publishing, students can create school or classroom announcements that need to be sent to parents, the community, or the school board. A classroom newsletter to parents offers students an opportunity to communicate with those outside the school community.

In more structured activities, students involved in team projects can be required to take notes and write up minutes for project meetings. In a construction technology class, students take turns taking the notes for a class, then writing them up as minutes. All science and technology lab classes should require students to maintain a journal, while technology classes should require students to read the specifications of the projects on which they work or write specifications for projects they develop on their own.

Students need to receive instruction in the following:

- organizing information for a feasibility study, white paper, position paper, and proposal
- writing persuasively for workplace audiences
- evaluating information to reach a conclusion and make a recommendation
- writing comparison/contrasts
- explaining and describing objects and processes for the lay public
- the conventions for writing a lab journal, the minutes of a meeting, E-mail, and journalistic news and feature writing
- newsletter writing and writing announcements
- using word processing and desktop publishing
- designing posters
- reading specifications
- *Robert's Rules of Order*

Students need practice in the following:

- writing white papers and position papers
- writing feasibility studies
- sending and receiving messages via E-mail
- writing articles for newsletters using word processing and desktop publishing
- writing announcements using word processing and desktop publishing
- designing and presenting posters
- writing and speaking to the general public
- taking notes at a meeting and writing them up in the form of minutes
- keeping a lab journal
- following specifications to create a product or process
- writing specifications for a product or process

Reading and Listening

In addition to providing our students with instruction in communicating orally, visually, and in writing, we need to provide them with instruction in reading the various documents and graphics and in listening during oral presentations and discussions.

Workplace documents are formatted so that readers can quickly and easily acquire the information they contain. Students need to learn how to locate this information through tables of contents, tables of figures, and indices, and through markers such as chapter titles, page numbers, and headings and subheadings. They also need to learn to engage in the five forms of reading behavior: skimming, scanning, searching, studying, and evaluating.

To give my students practice in engaging in this type of reading, I establish a scenario in which they assume the role of an employee in a specific division who has been asked by his supervisor to read a one-hundred-page report, and then write a memo explaining the effect of the report on his division. The supervisor needs the report within a fifteen-minute period. The only way the students can accomplish this task in the given time period is to scan the Executive Summary to determine if any of the major recommendations relate to their particular divisions. If so, by using the Table of Contents, they can turn to the section in the report that relates to those recommendations and, by skimming through the information, determine the effects on their respective divisions.

In teaching reading skills, we need to provide some accompanying writing skills. In addition to providing students with practice in reading in the workplace, the activity above gives them practice in writing a summary, a rhetorical form they need to learn as they learn to read a document. Furthermore, we need to teach students how to take notes. Most students simply copy the notes we place on a blackboard or, in listening to us lecture, they quote us verbatim when they notice our tone indicates an important fact or concept. They need to learn how to paraphrase what we say as well as to translate our statements into statements that have meaning for them. Finally, we need to teach them to annotate their readings. Because many schools only lend students their books, requiring that they be returned at the end of the school year, students are told not to write in the pages. However, learning to make notes in the margins, to write a synopsis of a chapter in the blank space at the beginning of a chapter, and to highlight important concepts in a text are methods for gathering information that students need to acquire. I often suggest students write in their books in pencil which can then be erased at the end of the term.

Students need practice in the following:

- reading various technical subgenres
- skimming, scanning, searching, understanding, and evaluating technical documents
- understanding how to read a document, depending on position, job, and purpose
- listening to oral presentations so they can respond to them
- listening in team meetings so they can analyze, synthesize, and evaluate the discussion
- taking notes, annotating reading materials, summarizing documents

Conclusion

By providing our students with instruction in a variety of workplace genres and subgenres, we can expand their repertoire of communication strategies, and provide them with the skills they need to voice their thoughts in the public forum of the workplace. It is their voices that will command attention to the ethics of doing business, to the preservation of the environment, and to the health and safety of their fellow workers.

Four

The Literature of Workplace English

I remember reading *Jane Eyre, Alice Adams,* and *Return of the Native* when I was young. I would sit in my bedroom, propped up against the pillows, the flowered spread under me, and read for hours. I never heard the clatter of dishes below as the dinner table was being set, or the slam of the front door as my father returned from work, or my mother's call to dinner. Neither the promise of hamburgers or fried chicken, and certainly not the liver on Wednesdays could entice me from Jane's search for food and shelter as she fled from Rochester's tortured admission of marriage.

Today, I lie in my bed, long past the time my husband, child, and Sam, the dog, have gone to sleep, the lamp next to me the only light in the darkened house, and read to solve a murder on Tony Hillerman's Navajo reservation or a puzzle in some techno-scientific world of Michael Crichton. For me it is still an escape for a moment from debates in English committee meetings, from worrying about a sixteen-year-old driving a car, from the increasing evidence of deterioration in the old dog's back legs.

It is this absorption into the world of the book that I see in my son's face as we read the *Chronicles of Narnia* together and return again and again to that scene in which they pass through the secret wardrobe into the land beyond. It is this magical piece of furniture that transports readers into another world that I want to give my students when I assign a book for them to read. But all too often, I am afraid, I have done the reverse: I have limited them to a static world of words without allowing them to taste and smell the story.

If we want our students, especially those enrolled in applied courses, to react more sensitively to the human condition and the environment in which we live as well as to become *literate* and to sample literary classics, then we need to provide them with the opportunity to become lost in the books we want them to read. In the remainder of this chapter we will examine ways to help them achieve this objective. We will discuss needed changes in our focus, approaches, and methods. We will also review our criteria for selecting the literary works we assign, and we will consider expanding our reading assignments to include workplace literature.

Changing Focus, Approach, and Methods

From an examination of the curriculums and the textbooks of most secondary English courses, we can infer that the goal of an English Department is to provide students with information about the literary genres of American, British, and world literature; to familiarize them with the major authors and their major works; and to help them recognize the themes and trends of the various periods. In other words, we want students to be literate in E.D. Hirsch's sense of cultural literacy, which is to possess the "basic [specific, communally shared] information needed to thrive in the modern world" (1987, xiii). In addition, we hope that students acquire an aesthetic appreciation for books, what Purves (1990) calls a "taste for good literature," and that they learn to enjoy reading in the same way that we enjoy losing ourselves in a novel by Tolstoy or Hemingway. Finally, we want our students to acquire a better understanding of the human condition, and develop values and a social awareness that result in increased sensitivity to the diverse needs of individuals in contemporary society (Rosenblatt 1978).

These objectives are as valid for students who do not plan to attend a four-year college as they are for those who do. However, according to a recent study by Applebee (1992), the focus of almost all courses in literature is not on cultural awareness, the human condition, and personal growth, but on the textual features of a work. Rather than engaging in a discussion of the motives that drove Sister Carrie, classes engage in critical analyses through a close reading of a text. This approach has hindered us from achieving our objectives with many students, especially those who are not in college prep, as attested to by their low grades, their failure to read books other than those assigned, and their reluctance to continue reading literature after they have completed their formal schooling. As one student explained, "I hate to read

judgments about the texts they read: "Though a free, uninhibited emotional reaction to a work of art or literature is an absolutely *necessary* condition of sound literary judgment, it is not...a *sufficient* condition....[The student] can begin to achieve a sound approach to literature only when he reflects upon his response to it...and when he goes on thoughtfully to modify, reject, or accept it" (88–89).

Activities and methods emanating from reader response theories have been very successful in engaging students in literature. These should include thinking aloud, oral interpretation, extended writing, writing in the personal mode, autobiographical responses, free writing, small group discussion, informal oral or written exploratory response, relating prior texts to current text, relating students attitudes to their responses, and sharing responses (Beach 1990). A large number of books and journal articles have been written suggesting activities of this sort for a wide range of literary works (Dyson 1989; Carlson and Sherrill 1988; Phelan 1990; Probst 1988).

Using these methods in a variety of combinations, we can develop activities that reflect students' learning styles as well as enable them to engage in the evocation and response phases of Nelms' model. We might ask students to work in groups, as professional writers do, to write a modern-day version of *Romeo and Juliet,* or to develop a story board for a daytime soap of the play, or, after watching the film version of *West Side Story,* to write a musical version of the Shakespearean tragedy. The latter is a good activity if there are a number of musically talented students in a class. Students might even decide to put on one of these "variations on a Shakespearean theme" for another class.

Jill Redmond, an English teacher at Portage High School in Indiana, developed a workplace English activity to get students involved with *MacBeth.* She gave students theatrical roles, such as set designer, props manager, costumer, and technical director, then assigned them tasks related to producing the plays. The designers had to deisgn sets reflecting the era's architecture and interior furnishings; the prop managers were required to create a menu for Banquo's feast, representing the kind of meal eaten by royalty in Scotland during the century in which the play occurred; and the costumers were expected to design the wearing apparel for the players based on the fashions of the day. The assignment allowed students to learn about the kinds of work theatre people do as well as to research the architecture, food, and fashion of a particular time.

By providing students with opportunities to read a broad section of texts, become involved with them, and respond to them, we are meeting some of the objectives we discussed at the beginning of this section. However, if we wish to broaden our students' worldviews and encourage them to question their values through analytical thinking and critical judgment, we need to engage them at least to some extent in the interpretation and criticism phases of Nelms' model.

Kelly Jackson, an English teacher at Summerville High School in South Carolina, developed the following activity in relation to her Workplace English course, to encourage students to think more deeply about *Lord of the Flies*.

> In *Lord of the Flies*, the plane-wrecked boys are in desperate need of team management skills. You are a team management consultant. In a business letter to the leaders, Jack and Ralph, suggest how team management could improve their situation. In making your suggestion, you will need to explain the concept of team management and indicate the communication skills they will need to carry it out. To persuade them that team management is the way to go, you will want to describe how several of their situations would have been improved. You can show them this by comparing and contrasting how events *were* and how they *could be* if they possessed the appropriate skills.

Reconsidering Texts

Adopting a different methodology, approach, and focus for teaching traditional literature is not the only change we need to make in our classrooms. We also need to reconsider the texts we teach. We need to determine whether we should continue to teach all of them, and, if we respond *no*, then we need to determine which ones to keep and which to eliminate. In the process, we need to be careful that we do not throw the baby out with the bath water. A well-balanced literature class should introduce students to three types of literature: traditional literary texts that are unrelated to the workplace; traditional literary texts that are workplace related; and workplace texts.

Traditional Literary Texts

All of us have our own favorite stories and poems that we want to introduce to our students. There are also texts that all of us believe should be taught if our students are to become culturally literate citizens, though each of our lists probably differs. Such texts as *Romeo and Juliet, Jane Eyre, Walden, Our Town*, and the poetry of Wordsworth, Dickens, and Eliot may fall into this category. In addition, there are those authors whom we have only recently brought into our classrooms—women authors, such as Nadine Gordimer and Margaret Atwood; African American authors, such as Ralph Ellison and Toni Morrison; Hispanic authors, like Jose Armas and Gabriel Garcia Marquez; and Asian authors, like Amy Tan and Maxine Hong Kingston—whose ideas and culture should be introduced to our students. There is no reason to stop teaching many of these, though we may need to weed our list a bit.

One criteria for weeding should be our students' readiness for the thematic material presented in a book. We need to consider whether our students are sufficiently mature to handle *King Lear,* "My Last Duchess," or even *Hamlet.* These works involve themes far beyond our students' experiences, and, thus, their understanding. Rosenblatt warns us not to "cram the classics down students' throats long before they are ready" and advises, "They will come to the classics at that point in their mental and emotional development when particular works will have particular significance for them" (257–58). At a point in their lives when they were examining organized religion, three students at Valparaiso High School in Indiana asked for copies of *Elmer Gantry* after watching the film in their English class.

By using a little imagination, we can also integrate these readings with workplace writing. Laura Walters, who found the set of activities in Figure 4–1 at a Tech-Prep Idea Exchange, has been asking students to draft a variety of workplace documents in relation to *Julius Caesar.*

Figure 4–1
Julius Caesar—Business Portfolio

Portfolio Requirements:

1. Three resumes (one for each chosen character), each with a cover letter, letter of request, and follow-up letter. Choose from the list of characters:

Julius Caesar	Marc Antony
Cassius	Marcus Brutus
Calpurnia	Portia
a Soothsayer	Artemidorus

2. Five memorandums (one each) from the following people:

   The soothsayer to Julius Caesar
   Marc Antony to the Roman people
   Cassius to Brutus
   Portia to Artemidorus
   Marc Antony to Brutus

3. Five in-house messages

4. Ten phone messages

   Five using the standard message form
   Five without the structure of the standard form

5. Three letters of complaint

Applying Traditional Texts to Workplace English

Some traditional texts lend themselves easily to being taught from the viewpoint of the workplace. Many of those included in high school anthologies are either set in the workplace, like Updike's "A & P"; depict characters whose work is very much a part of their fate, like Fontine in *Les Miserables*; or involve workplace-related themes, like Pirsig's *Zen and the Art of Motorcycle Maintenance*. Some, like Dickens' *Hard Times* and Hemingway's *Old Man and the Sea*, encompass all of these.

These texts can be incorporated into a course in a number of ways: They might be taught as a single unit on the workplace, or they might be integrated into our traditional units with our other texts. For example, Twain's personal narrative, *Life on the Mississippi*, might be included in a unit on nineteenth-century American literature; Updike's short story, "A & P," might be included in a unit on loss of innocence; and Dicken's fictional commentary, *Hard Times*, in a unit on the novel.

As we select various texts, we need to determine whether to assign a work to be read aesthetically or efferently. Our decisions on the type of reading we wish our students to do should drive our lessons, our methods, and our assessments. While the predominant stance we want students to take in reading books such as *Hard Times* and *The Old Man and the Sea* is aesthetic, we know they will acquire some information about child labor and fishing respectively. In like manner, while we may want students to read texts such as Upton Sinclair's novel, *The Jungle*, or Studs Terkel's nonfiction piece, *Working*, efferently, we know that they can also engage in an aesthetic experience in relation to the author's descriptive passages and sympathetically drawn characters. As students engage in efferent reading, they will acquire information about the workplace; as they engage in aesthetic reading, their attitudes toward various aspects of the workplace, their sensitivity toward the workers in it, and their understanding of their role as workers will develop. By introducing students to the world of work as it is depicted in literature, students can receive an historical perspective of the workplace, obtain a kaleidoscopic view of the jobs and trades people follow, and acquire some schemata for technical and scientific prose.

A Historical Perspective. Literature allows us to provide students with fascinating accounts of the world of work at different stages of our history. The workplace of the fourteenth century is vividly painted by Chaucer in his *Canterbury Tales*. This picaresque series of stories provides us with an opportunity to introduce students to the kinds of work in which people were involved in the Middle Ages, i.e., millers, pardoners, clerks, merchants, physicians, shipmen, cooks, reeves, alchemists, and manciples. *Tales* also offers an opportunity for students to study the changes that the workplace has undergone over the centuries. Some of the pilgrims' vocations no longer exist, e.g., alchemists, while others have different nomenclature, e.g., a reeve is known today as a bailiff or steward, and a manciple is known as a purchasing agent.

The human consequences of the industrial revolution in nineteenth-century Europe are portrayed through the literature of such authors as Charles Dickens, Victor Hugo, and William Makepiece Thackeray. By reading the stories of these authors, students can walk about the bleak, urbanized, and industrialized landscape in which the workers, and especially the women and children, toil from darkness to darkness in twelve-hour shifts. Through the critiques of industrialization in America, emanating from such authors as Upton Sinclair and Frank Norris, students can develop a humane response to the making of America.

By reading excerpts from Upton Sinclair's novel, *The Jungle* (1906), which castigates the meat-packing industry, students can envision the stinking, monotonous, and dreary conditions in which men, women, and children lived and worked at the turn of the century:

> The sausage room was an interesting place to visit, for two or three minutes...the machines were perhaps the most wonderful things in the entire plant. Presumably sausages were once chopped and stuffed by hand, and if so it would be interesting to know how many workers had been displaced by these inventions. On one side of the room were the hoppers, into which men shovelled loads of meat and wheelbarrows full of spices; in these great bowls were whirling knives that made two thousand revolutions a minute, and when the meat was ground fine and adulterated with potato flour and well mixed with water, it was forced to the stuffing machines on the other side of the room. The latter were tended by women: there was a sort of spout, like the nozzle of a hose, and one of the women would take a long string of 'casing' and put the end over the nozzle and then work the whole thing on, as one works on the finger of a tight glove. This string would be twenty or thirty feet long, but the woman would have it all on in a jiffy; and when she had several on, she would press a lever, and a stream of sausage meat would be shot out, taking the casing with it as it came. Thus one might stand and see appear, miraculously born from the machine, a wriggling snake of sausage of incredible length. In front was a big pan which caught these creatures, and two more women who seized them as fast as they appeared and twisted them into links....for all that the woman had to give a single turn of the wrist; and in some miraculous way she contrived to give it so that instead of an endless chain of sausages, one after another, there grew under her hands a bunch of strings, all dangling from a single centre. It was quite like the feat of a prestidigitator—for the woman worked so fast that the eye could literally not follow her, and there was only a

mist of motion, and tangle after tangle of sausages appearing. In the midst of the mist, however, a visitor would suddenly notice the tense set face, with the two wrinkles graven in the forehead, and the ghastly pallor of the cheeks....The woman...stayed right there—hour after hour, day after day, year after year, twisting sausage links and racing with death. It was piecework and she was apt to have a family to keep alive; and stern and ruthless economic laws had arranged it that she could only do this by working just as she did, with all her soul upon her work. (159–161)

Through Frank Norris' novel, *The Octopus* ([1901], 1986), in which the author chronicles the conflicts between land and capital, freedom and monopoly, and labor and management, the public and the trust (corporation) (Starr 1986, xiv), students can envision the giant, thunderous machines that industrialized the farmlands. Perceiving the farm as an outdoor factory, Norris presents students with a picture of farmers as corporate executives, rather than as lovers of the earth as depicted in novels by such authors as Willa Cather. By reading scenes such as the one below, in which the machines, rather than the earth or the farmer are the focus, students from urban and suburban areas can confront the writer's view of the modern farm.

The ploughs, thirty-five in number, each drawn by its team of ten, stretched in an interminable line, nearly a quarter of a mile in length, behind and ahead...They were arranged, as it were, *en echelon*, not in file—not one directly behind the other, but each succeeding plough its own width farther in the field than the one in front of it. Each of these ploughs held five shears, so that when the entire company was in motion, one hundred and seventy-five furrows were made at the same instant. At a distance, the ploughs resembled a great column of field artillery. Each driver was in his place, his glance alternating between his horses and the foreman nearest at hand. Suddenly, from a distance at the head of the line, came the shrill trilling of a whistle. The signal was repeated, whistle answering whistle, till the sounds lost themselves in the distance. At once the line of ploughs lost its immobility, moving forward, getting slowly under way, the horses straining in the races. A prolonged movement rippled from team to team, disengaging in its passage a multitude of sounds—the click of buckles, the creak of straining leather, the subdued clash of machinery, the cracking of whips, the deep breathing of nearly four hundred horses, the abrupt commands and cries of the drivers, and last of all, the prolonged, soothing murmur of the thick brown earth turning steadily from the multitude of advancing shears. (127–28)

Picking up where Norris and Sinclair leave off, twentieth-century authors, such as Isaac Asimov, George Orwell, and Aldous Huxley, use science fiction to examine the future consequences of industrialization.

A Kaleidoscopic View. In altering our focus from text to response in teaching literature, we can provide students with an introduction to the workplace in its broadest sense. Through literature, our students can enter the world of work. They can walk through the heavy metal doors of a manufacturing plant, peek into the cubicles of an office building, observe the intricately equipped rooms of health care facilities, and walk down the halls of structures where criminal justice is meted out. They can gain insights into the lives and lifestyles of the workers as they interact with each other, their families, and society. And they can observe the consequences of the various trades and the technologies involved in those trades on the environment and on the lives of others. They can begin to construct a schema for the workplace and develop a set of ethical standards for their own work, as well as visualize the context in which workplace communication takes place.

A large number of texts provide students with insights into the world of work, through their depiction of the lifestyles people lead as they pursue careers or simply try to survive. Novels such as *The Man in the Gray Flannel Suit* and Updike's *Rabbit, Run*, and dramas, such as Arthur Miller's *Death of a Salesman* and *Memory of Two Mondays*, provide vivid characterizations of men working in the middle of the twentieth century. Studs Terkel's books provide nonfiction counterparts to these texts, with their powerful descriptions of real people who actually live and survive in the workplace. Students can respond to the plight of working women in an historical context through books, such as Dreiser's *Sister Carrie*, Hugo's *Les Miserables*, and Tarkington's *Alice Adams*. A more recent picture is created by Marge Piercy in "Gone to Soldiers," a portrait of working women during and after World War II. Wasserman's drama, *The Heidi Chronicles*, produced on Broadway and made into a cable TV movie, allows students to respond to the dilemmas faced by women today as they achieve equality with men in the workplace.

Literature also provides students with views into a wide variety of industries. Arthur Hailey's books offer an inside look at companies ranging from those involved with automobile production to those engaged in the financial markets to those generating and distributing electric power. Michael Crichton provides a glance into the computer industry in *Disclosure*.

Many texts offer students an opportunity to examine ethical issues related to the workplace. Book VI of *Piers the Ploughman*, written in the fourteenth century, which is specifically devoted to work, offers a means to introduce the concept of "work or go hungry," a theme that is repeated in such twentieth-century books as Steinbeck's *Grapes of Wrath* and Hemingway's *The Old Man and the Sea*. The latter two books, as well as St. Exupery's *Night Flight*, provide concrete examples of Pirsig's philosophy of work as an end in itself and a means of self-actualization. All of these offer a starting point for discussions related to the social welfare programs initiated by President Franklin D. Roosevelt, in his efforts to alleviate the effects of the Great Depression. The excerpt below, written in 1952, is from the memoirs of President Herbert Hoover. It concerns Hoover's attempts to raise monies for the rehabilitation of the lower Mississippi region, where he was sent in 1927 as Secretary of Commerce under President Calvin Coolidge. The excerpt includes Hoover's reaction to Roosevelt's introduction of the welfare program.

> As at this time we all believed in self-help, I financed the operation by three actions. We put on a Red Cross drive by radio from the flood area, and raised $15,000,000. I secured $1,000,000 from the Rockefeller Foundation to finance the after-flood campaign of sanitation to be matched by equal contributions from the counties. We organized a nonprofit organization through the United States Chamber of Congress to provide $10,000,000 of loans at low rates, for rehabilitation, every cent of which was paid back. But those were the days when citizens were expected to take care of one another in time of disaster and it had not occurred to them that the Federal Government should do it. (126)

Students can find the philosophic bases of many contemporary economic problems in a variety of historic literary texts. *The Merchant of Venice* involves the problem of debt and usury, a subject which Shakespeare touches on again in *Hamlet*, in Polonius' "Neither a borrower nor a lender be" speech to Laertes. The topic offers an opportunity for students to relate the texts they're reading to the country's economic situation, which has been depicted as being built on credit and burdened with debt. Students should be able to relate their prior knowledge of credit to the text to help them understand it. They should also be able to expand their knowledge and attitudes about credit by relating the text to their experiences.

Discussions related to *Merchant* also provide an opportunity to examine usury from an historical perspective. By reading Dickens' novel, *Oliver Twist*, written in the nineteenth century, and Alex Hailey's novel on banking, written in the mid-twentieth century, students have an opportunity to learn about how a credit society operates. And by viewing any one of the many contemporary films, such as *It's a Wonderful Life*, or *The Stars Fell on Henrietta*, that deal with borrowing money to start a business or to keep a business going, students can see and respond to the human consequences of a "credit society."

Students also have an opportunity to respond to the complexities of various ethical dilemmas involving the workplace through several contemporary texts. Michael Crichton's *Disclosure* grapples with one of the major issues of the 1990s, sexual harassment, and Arthur Hailey's *Wheels* and *Power* allow students to respond to issues such as diversity and disability. William Barrett's short story, "Senõr Payroll," combines American ethics with Hispanic culture; Gabriel Garcia Marquez's "Balthazar's Marvelous Afternoon" extends the ethics of business to encompass the ethics of mankind; and Updike's "A & P" offers an opportunity for students to respond to one high school students' ethical decision.

A Taste of Technical and Scientific Prose. Through adventure stories, science fiction, and spy novels, which are often filled with information about mechanical devices, technological processes, and scientific discoveries, we can provide students with opportunities to read well-written technical and scientific prose. Students can find a variety of technical, medical, and scientific descriptions in Chaucer's *Canterbury Tales*. The relationship between astronomy and medicine as it was practiced in medieval times is specifically described in the "Doctor of Physics" tale.

Jules Verne's *Travels to the Center of the Earth* and *Twenty Thousand Leagues under the Sea* and Herman Melville's *Moby Dick* include classic examples of technical and scientific prose. These books fuse reading for pleasure (aesthetic reading) with reading for information (efferent reading), providing students with a new literary genre, which many students may find contains more interesting texts than those books requiring a purely aesthetic reading, such as the novels of George Eliot or Nathaniel Hawthorne.

Verne's description of the Nautilus in *Twenty Thousand Leagues Under the Sea* serves as a model description of a mechanism.

> The *Nautilus* is composed of two hulls, one inside, the other outside, joined by T-shaped irons, which render it very strong. Indeed, owing to this cellular arrangement it resists like a block, as if it were solid. Its sides cannot yield; it coheres spontaneously, and not by the closeness of its rivets; and the homogeneity of its construction, due to the perfect union of the materials, enables it to defy the roughest seas.
>
> These two hulls are composed of steel plates, whose density is from .7 to .8 that of water. The first is not less than two inches and a half thick, and weighs 394 tons. The second envelope, the keel, twenty inches high and ten thick, weighs along sixty-two tons. The engine, the ballast, the several accessories and apparatus appendages, the partitions and bulkheads, weigh 961.62 tons....
>
> When the *Nautilus* is afloat,...one-tenth is out of the water. Now if I have made reservoirs of a size equal to this, or capable of holding 150 tons, and if I fill them with water, the boat, weighing then 1507 tons, will be completely immersed...These reservoirs are in the lower parts of the *Nautilus*. I turn on taps and they fill, and the vessel sinks that had just been level with the surface. ([1873] 1993, 95)

The specific details and technical terminology provide the story with an authentic voice so that the reader can easily "suspend disbelief" and accept the information as plausible. In fact, though the book was written before a modern submarine was developed, Verne's description is very close to that of one, and comes very near the description of a Russian submarine, described by Tom Clancy in his novel, *The Hunt for Red October*, written over a century after Verne wrote his book:

> A very large vessel, about 650 feet long, a beam of roughly 85 feet, and an estimated submerged displacement of 32,000 tons....her hull is oblate. Instead of being cylindrical like ours, it is flattened out markedly top and bottom. (1984, 101–102)

In other descriptions of the Russian sub, Clancy's description parallels Verne's, referring to the "double hull" (10) and to the use of tanks to sink the craft (8).

While Verne's descriptions are creative and purely speculative, the submarine being no more than an idea, Melville's descriptions in *Moby Dick* ([1851] 1983) are based on actual knowledge, garnered from his own sailing experiences. In his chapter, "Cetology," Melville is the epitome of the contemporary scientific writer; his description is detailed, impersonal, and without literary rhetorical devices.

> A monster which, by the various names of Fin-Back, Tall-Spout, and Long-John, has been seen almost in every sea and is commonly the whale whose distant jet is so often descried by passengers crossing the Atlantic, in the New York packet-tracks. In the length he attains, and in his baleen, the fin-back resembles the right whale, but is of a less portly girth, and a lighter color, approaching to olive. His great lips present a cable-like aspect, formed by the intertwisting, slanting folds of large wrinkles. His grand distinguishing feature, the fin, from which he derives his name, is often a conspicuous object. This fin is some three or four feet long, growing vertically from the hinder part of the back, of an angular shape and with a very sharp pointed end. (939)

In contrast, in his chapter "The Right Whale's Head," Melville becomes more poetic, using metaphorical language to enhance his description, and giving students an opportunity to hear scientific terms engage in a "dance of words" that conjures up exotic images:

> The noble Sperm Whale's head may be compared to a Roman war-chariot....As you come nearer to this great head it begins to assume different aspects, according to your point of view. If you stand on the summit and look at these two *f*-shaped spout-holes, you would take the whole head for an enormous bass-viol, and these spiracles, the aperatures in its sounding board. Then again, if you fix your eye upon this strange, crested, comb-like incrustation on the top of the mass— this green, barnacled thing, which the Greenlanders call the "crown,"

and the Southern fishers the "bonnet" of the Right Whale; fixing your
eyes solely on this, you would take the head for the trunk of some
huge oak, with a bird's nest in its crotch. (1149)

A number of contemporary authors also provide exemplary models of
process descriptions and definitions of objects, two key rhetorical
devices required in workplace English. Tom Clancy's descriptions of
nuclear power and supercomputers in *The Hunt for Red October* and
Michael Crichton's descriptions of genetic tinkering in *Jurassic Park*
and virtual reality software in *Disclosure* are excellent examples of
writing about technical topics for the general public. Crichton's
Andromeda Strain even includes models of various technical documents, including memoranda and progress reports, providing students
with opportunities not only to read these documents, but to discover
how they function in a work environment.

Workplace Literature

In addition to the literature traditionally taught in the classroom, a
great deal of workplace literature exists with which students ought to
become familiar. Just as we introduce students to such ancient literary
texts as *Beowulf,* so that they have a greater appreciation of their literary heritage, we also need to acquaint them with the forerunners of
the workplace documents they will be reading and writing once they
enter the workforce. A large number of texts that were written hundreds, even thousands, of years ago serve as the precursors of the documents written today. Students should have an opportunity to read
some of the technical and scientific documents that were broadly cir-
culated in the sixteenth century, after the invention of the printing
press made the copying and distribution of such information simpler.
Many of these documents, like the ones below, were in the form of
recipes, instructions for midwives, and directions for farming that provided citizens with basic household information on cooking meats,
caring for newborns, and tilling land.

for to make chickens in mushy

To make chickens in mushy/take small chickens chopped and boil
them in sweet broth and wine and put there parcely and sage and pow-
der of pepper or grains and color it with saffron/then take white of eggs
and ale drawn through a cloth and put there and stir it well together
and put there an ounce of ginger and when it beginneth to boil set it
from the fire and serve it. (Cited in Tebeaux and Lay 1992, 198)

A tumor...is a prominence or protuberance in the bodie. And from
hence, the Latine words uncus a crooke or hooke, and aduncus,
bended or crooked, are derived....For humors, which cause Apostemes,

come from the veines, and so leaving ther own natural receptackle, seat themselves in other parts of the body, being dependant and weake. And Surgeons commonly call Tumors where in there is a collection of matter Apostemes. (Cited in Tebeaux and Lay 1992, 200)

If you determine to manure the whole site, this is your way: dig a trench half a yard deep, all along the Lower (if there be a Lower) side of your Orchard plot, casting up all the earth on the inner side, and fill the same with good earth, hot, and tender muck, and make such an other Trench, and fill the same, as the first and so the third, and so throughout your ground. And by this meanes your plot shall be fertile for your life. (Cited in Tebeaux and Lay 1992, 205)

In addition to these minor historic documents, students should be introduced to some of the technical and scientific texts that have become classics because of their influence on events.

Historic Texts. One of the best known historical documents is Thucydides' description of the plague, written in 430 B.C. (1934). The plague occurred during the Peloponnesian Wars and was probably a major cause of the defeat of the Greek army by the Spartans. Thucydides' presentation of patients' symptoms was so detailed and precise that, in 1987, 2,500 years after the document was written, two doctors in Minneapolis were able to identify the specific disease as a type of influenza complicated by Toxic Shock Syndrome (Bruce 1987). The following excerpt from Thucydides provides students with an exemplary model of a scientific description:

People in good health were all of a sudden attacked by violent heats in the head, and redness and inflammation in the eyes, the inward parts, such as the throat or tongue, becoming bloody and emitting an unnatural and fetid breath. (110)

Thucydides' text is not the only historic document to have implications for the modern world. Students can read Vitruvius' instructions for building the walls of Rome, written in 27 B.C. (Pollio 1960) and Agricola's discourse on mining, written in 1556 (1950).

Vitruvius wrote *De Architectura (Ten Books of Architecture)* (1960) for future architects, so that the classical tradition in the design of Rome's temples and public buildings would be preserved after he was gone. The book served as a guide to Roman architects throughout the period and well into the Renaissance, influencing the renowned sixteenth-century neoclassic architect Palladio. Our knowledge of how the two-tiered Roman walls were built comes from this manual. The manual also contains information on building the Roman aqueducts and on tunneling through mountains. The sturdy gray stone bridges spanning Philadelphia's Schuylkill river, immortalized by the painter

Thomas Eakins, were based on Vitruvius' directions in *De Architectura*, excerpted below:

> To lay the foundations for the towers and walls, dig down to solid bottom, if it can be found, and lay them, therein, going as deep as the magnitude of the proposed work seems to require. They should be much thicker than the part of the walls that will appear above ground and their structure should be as solid as it can possibly be laid. (21–22)

Vitruvius' directions include both homespun and technical advice. The following excerpt provides a wonderful opportunity to conduct a class discussion on the effects of land pollution on our living conditions, and on the responsibility of industry to protect citizens from poisons leaching into their lands and rivers. It also offers an opportunity to discuss the responsibilities of technicians to those who will use their products and services:

> I cannot too strongly insist upon the need of a return to the method of old times. Our ancestors, when about to build a town or an army post, sacrificed some of the cattle that were wont to feed on the site proposed and examined their livers. If the livers of the first victims were dark-coloured or abnormal, they sacrificed others to see whether the fault was due to disease or their food. They never began to build defensive works in a place until after they had made many such trials and satisfied themselves that good water and food had made the liver sound and firm. If they continued to find it abnormal, they argued from this that the food and water supply found in such a place would be just as unhealthy for man, and so they moved away and changed to another neighbourhood, healthfulness being their chief object. (20)

Agricola's *De Re Metallica* was written to provide information and instructions in the art of metalworking, and was used as a textbook. In addition to providing an example of an early instructional manual, it offers an opportunity for class discussions on industry's responsibilities to its workers. In Agricola's discussion of underground mining, he is aware of workplace safety and directs those constructing the mines to beware of creating hazards:

> Now when a miner discovers a *vera profunda*, he begins sinking a shaft and above it sets up a windlass, and builds a shed over the shaft to prevent the rain from falling in, lest the men who turn the windlass be numbed by the cold or troubled by the rain....Next to the shaft-house another house is built where the mine foreman and the other workmen dwell....[B]ecause boys and other living things fall into the shafts, most miners deliberately place one house apart from the other, or at least separate them by a wall. (102)

These documents offer us an opportunity to provide students with an appreciation of how written forms of communication provide people with information needed at the time they are written, and also preserve the culture and knowledge of the past so that it can be drawn upon in the future.

Thus, the documents we write today will inform future generations about our knowledge and culture. The Environmental Impact Study for the Manhattan African Slave Burial Ground is an example. The African Slave Burial Ground was discovered in the early 1990s after construction workers began excavation work to build a new federal courthouse in downtown Manhattan. Prior to engaging in any construction, all contractors must submit an Environmental Impact Statement that indicates whether the construction or the work in which the building will be involved will create environmental pollution or will disturb any historical or archaeological site. The contractors knew that a burial ground had existed at one time under the site, but they felt that because other buildings had been built there, the remains had been destroyed long ago. When the burial ground was found to be intact, and, in fact, was the largest extant slave burial ground in the North, construction was halted and the contractors were required to develop a document called a research design that would outline their plans for dealing with the site and the remains.

The document not only demonstrates how our past informs our present, but it also serves as a model of a white paper, the business equivalent of a research or term paper, as you can see from the following excerpt. The writer of the research design provides a history of the site so readers recognize its significance and understand the reason the site should not be destroyed. Thus, research papers, which are not usually connected with anything that appears relevant to students, may suddenly take on a new importance as they see them in relation to a real purpose. Students also have an opportunity to see how sources are cited and referenced, something they are asked to do but seldom see. By reading such an excerpt, they can begin to develop a schema for a research or white paper.

> The streets bounding the Broadway Block were not laid out until c. 1784–1795. Before that, the southern portion of the block, which was outside the city's palisade, had been used by New York City's African community as a burial ground. The "Negros Burial Ground" is clearly marked on a historic map dating to the mid-1700s.
>
> By most accounts the burial ground was being used as a final resting place for Africans, slaves and free people at least as early as 1712. Valentine's *Manual* provides one of the few known descriptions of the burial ground:
>
> > Beyond the commons lay what in the earliest settlement of the town had been appropriated as a burial place for Negroes, slave and free. It was a desolate, unappropriated

spot, descending with a gentle declivity towards a ravine which led to the Kalkhook pond. The Negroes in this city were, both in the Dutch and English colonial times, a proscribed and detested race....Many of them were native Africans, imported hither in slave ships, and retaining their native superstitions and burial customs, mummeries and outcries....So little seems to have been thought of the race that not even a dedication of their burial-place was made by the church authorities, or any others who might reasonably be supposed to have any interest in such a matter. The lands were unappropriated, and though within convenient distance from the city, the locality was unattractive and desolate, so that by permission the slave population were allowed to inter their dead there.

The Dutch West Indies Company was responsible for bringing the first enslaved Africans to Manhattan Island where, in 1625, the monopoly trading enterprise established the colonial settlement called New Amsterdam. In 1626 one of the company's vessels carried eleven enslaved Africans to the Dutch outpost. The names of several members of this inaugural shipment of human cargo—for example, Paulo Angola, Simon Congo, Anthony Portuguis, and Peter Santomee—suggest that before they were removed to New Amsterdam the enslaved Africans had lived in various slave societies along the Atlantic littoral—in the Congo-Angola region of Africa, in Sao Tomé, and perhaps in Portugal.

In 1628 a vessel of the Dutch company brought three enslaved African women to Manhattan. Although there is no explicit evidence that suggests the company intended to enter the business of breeding slaves, its records indicate that these women had been purchased, as the company's clerk put it, "for the comfort of the company's Negro men." Over the years, some enslaved Africans managed to establish stable families whose conjugal and consanguineal bonds the Dutch Reformed Church sanctioned through its marriage and baptismal ceremonies. This is not to say that the Dutch created a benign slave regime. However much the Dutch clerics professed their concern for the fate of the souls of Africans in the afterlife, they did little to ameliorate the slaves' conditions on earth.

Contemporary Documents

While some contemporary documents provide eloquent models of workplace texts, others attest to the consequences of workplace communication gone awry. Three national tragedies have been partially caused by miscommunication: the Three Mile Island (TMI) nuclear accident; the space shuttle Challenger disaster; and the Chicago flood. Students can read case studies of these events, including the actual correspondence written by the various participants. They can read the readers' written responses to memoranda and letters they received and discover how readers interpreted or failed to understand the messages being sent. Students can also acquire additional insights into the incidents. Environmentalist Barry Commoner, in his book, *The Politics of Energy*, describes his reaction to the nuclear accident at Three Mile Island in an emotional discussion of its ethical and economic consequences.

The Human Factor

Because the style of technical and scientific texts is impersonal, the humane aspects of the topics under discussion may be omitted. The result is a dehumanization of technical and scientific documents.

By contrasting fictional texts with technical or scientific ones, students can readily recognize the failure of the technical documents to present the human element. For example, in contrast to Thucydides impersonal description of the plague of Athens, Defoe mixes scientific and fictional techniques in his novel, *Journal of the Plague Year* ([1722] 1969), to present a spine-tingling picture of the London plague of 1665, in which readers can feel the fear and hear the death throes of the victims:

> A casement violently opened just over my head, and a woman gave three frightful screeches, and then cried, "Oh! death, death, death!" in a most inimitable tone, and which struck me with horror and a chilliness in my very blood. There was nobody to be seen in the whole street, neither did any of the windows open, for people had no curiosity now in any case, nor could anybody help one another, so I went on....
>
> It is impossible to know the infected People from the sound; or that the infected People should perfectly know themselves: I knew a Man who conversed freely in London all the Season of the Plague in 1665, and kept to him an Antidote or Cordial, on purpose to take when he thought himself in any Danger, and he had such a Rule to know, or have a warning of the Danger by, as indeed I never met with before or since, how far it may be depended on I know not: He had a Wound in his Leg, and whenever he came among any People that were not sound, and the Infection began to affect him, he said he could know it by that Signal (viz) That his Wound in his Leg would smart, and look pale and white, so as soon as ever he felt it smart, it was time for him to withdraw, or to take care of himself, taking his Drink, which he always carried about him for that Purpose. (191–92)

Fiction is not the only genre in which writers can display empathy with society. Students should have an opportunity to read documents that imply a sensitivity to the human condition, while simultaneously presenting scientific or technical information so that they can realize such a combination of viewpoints is possible. Such an account is presented by Herbert Hoover in his memoirs of the 1927 Mississippi flood. Hoover is as sensitive to the pathos of the human comedy as he is precise in his presentation of the technical information he has gathered:

> For rescue work we took over some forty river steamers and attached to each of them a flotilla of small boats under the direction of Coast Guardsmen. As the motorboats we could assemble proved insufficient, the sawmills up and down the river made me 1,000 rough boats in ten days. I rented 1,000 outboard motors from the manufacturers, which we were to return. (But after it was all over we could find only 120 motors. Undoubtedly every fisherman in the territory motorized his transportation.) (125–26)

Although students need to learn to present information factually, they need to keep in mind the effects of topics on human beings, and recognize the consequences to humanity. Taken to extremes, technical writing can be used to dehumanize society as is exemplified in the following odious memorandum written by a Nazi officer recommending changes to the gas vans being used at a concentration camp during World War II. The officer avoids mentioning the victims as much as possible. When he does refer to them, he uses sales terms, calling them "pieces" and "merchandise."

Geheime Reichssache Memo

Berlin, June 5, 1942

Changes for special vehicles now in service at Kulmhof (Chelmno)

Since December, 1941, ninety-seven thousand have been processed by the three vehicles in service, with no major incident. In the light of observations made so far, however, the following technical changes are needed.

The vans' normal load is usually nine per square yard. In Saurer vehicles, which are very spacious, maximum use of space is impossible, not because of any possible overload, but because loading to full capacity would affect the vehicle's stability. So reduction of the load space seems necessary. It must absolutely be reduced by a yard, instead of trying to solve the problem, as hitherto, by reducing the number of pieces loaded. Besides this extends the operating time, as the empty void must also be filled with carbon monoxide. On the other hand, if the load space is reduced, and the vehicle is packed solid, the operating time can be considerably shortened. The manufacturer told us during a discussion that reducing the size of the van's rear would throw it badly off balance. . . . In fact the balance is automatically restored, because the merchandise aboard displays during the operation a natural tendency to rush to the rear doors. . . . So the front axle is not overloaded.

Students need to be careful that they do not dehumanize their topic in their efforts to objectify their data as they engage in technical writing. They also need to learn to read technical documents as skeptically as they read advertisements. They should always think about the effects of technology on the planet and on those who inhabit it as they read about a new product or process. Therefore a unit in advertising might include brochures about technical products.

Integrating Workplace Literature into the Traditional English Curriculum

In this chapter I have been arguing for expanding the English curriculum to include workplace documents. The challenge is finding time for these texts in a course that is already too full. However, there are some ways that we can make room in the present curriculum without watering it down.

One way to provide time for reading workplace literature is to reduce the quantity of traditional literary works we assign. For example, in one reading series, sixteen entries are listed under the short story unit, in which the focus is on plot, characterization, setting, point of view, and theme. Another fifteen short stories are listed under the short fiction unit, in which the focus is on irony, symbolism, stereotypes, and mood. It would appear that all nine concepts could be taught by reading no more than three to five of the thirty-one stories listed. Certainly, Guy de Maupassant's short story "The Necklace," which is listed under the irony section of the short fiction unit, not only provides a vehicle for teaching irony, but also provides an opportunity to teach plot, point of view, theme, symbolism, and mood. We might also think about whether we really need to teach *all* of these aspects of literature. Perhaps we could eliminate mood, irony, or symbolism.

In addition to reducing the number of works that students are required to read, it is also possible to use methods that reduce the amount of time required to teach various texts. For example, many anthologies include *The Diary of Anne Frank* or *The Miracle Worker* as examples of drama. These plays were written to be seen and heard, not to be read. They were included in anthologies because, until recently, there was no way students could see and hear them. Today, however, with easy access to audio- and videotapes and VCRs, students can watch excellent productions of them. Not including pre- and post-reading lessons, teaching a drama by requiring students to read a play may take at least five days, while simply watching a play may take no more than three days.

Another method for reducing the amount of time required for teaching a unit is to provide students with the opportunity to teach each other in small group work, which Beach (1990) suggests as an effective technique for literature instruction. If you assign five short stories for all members of a class to read, it will probably take five days to cover five stories. However, by using small group work, you can shorten the time to less than three days. One story can be assigned to the entire class for reading and discussion. The class can then be divided into small groups of five with each person in a group assigned a different story. Students can then take turns discussing the specific story each of them has read. This activity can be repeated a second time. Thus, within three, rather than five, periods, students will have acquired knowledge of eleven stories, three in depth. And they will have gained some skill at summarizing and in making oral presentations.

We can further reduce the amount of time spent on a traditional literary unit by eliminating objectives that are not appropriate for these students. For example, one textbook on American Literature lists forty-nine items, including anastrophe, heroic couplet, metonymy, slant rhyme, and synecdoche, under the objective: "Students will understand and be able to apply to their reading the following literary terms." There is little reason for these students to know and apply the five terms listed above. In addition, one can question their need to recognize and name such aspects of literature as allusion, alliteration, consonance, assonance, and extended metaphor. In no way does this objective reflect the objectives we discussed at the beginning of this chapter. However, if teaching students to recognize irony will increase their understanding of a story or essay so that they can engage more successfully in Nelms' evocation and response phases, then irony as a rhetorical device should be taught when stories such as De Maupassant's "The Necklace" or Swift's "Modest Proposal" are assigned. It is the *story* that should drive the instructional lessons, rather than the *lessons* determining the story.

But what of the rhetorical devices and texts we omit? Will college literature teachers expect our students to have read them, or to know the various devices? The truth of the matter is that we can't teach it all. We need to establish a set of criteria that can provide a basis for selecting from among the thirty-one short stories or the twenty poems included in an anthology. Such criteria might include the frequency with which a book is cited in other works, a book's ability to represent a specific author, to provide a vehicle to achieve a major objective, or to offer students a view of the world to which they can respond. A text should not be taught simply because it is in an anthology. The works that we select must necessarily be based on our judgment as teachers of literature. Some of our decisions will reflect those of our colleagues, others will not.

Conclusion

By expanding the traditional English course to include applied English, we are enriching our curriculum. When the writing is done well, workplace and traditional literary texts merge to form documents of both aesthetic and informational value. The late anthropologist Loren Eiseley commingled the scientific discourse inherent in his field with the elegance of poetic form to reach beyond the specific data of anthropology and create texts that reflect the condition of humankind:

Why Did They Go?

Why did they go, why did they go away—
plesiosaurs, fish-reptiles, pterodactyls of the air,
tricerotops beneath an armored shield and frills of thorn,
tyrannosaurs with little withered hands, but jaws more huge than
        anything that stalks the modern world—
why did they go?
    Were they
        in the egg vulnerable?
But then there trotted after, through green glades,
            bones the size of collies,
            gracefully stepping cats
with teeth like knives. They roared, they roared,
            and then they struck,
    finding the jugular like adept assassins,
    searching through aeons till they came upon, in turn,
    camels, musk-oxen, antelope and deer,
also the throats of bison heavy-maned with giant horns.
Mammoth, mastodon, beyond the knives of even such as these,
            they also ebbed away as the ice ebbed,
as the first wolves grew scarcer, and as man, naked, shook
his first flint-headed spear that had at last outsprung
the giant cats. Why did they go, through eras, centuries, the strong,
                                    the strongest?

Five

The Fusion of Technology and Aesthetics in Workplace English

The root word for technology, techne, *originally meant "art." The ancient Greeks never separated art from manufacture in their minds, and so never developed separate words for them.*

(Pirsig 1976, 283)

Workplace and literary genres have not always been the separate entities they have become. Today we may question the appropriateness of teaching workplace documents in an English or liberal arts curriculum because they appear to be devoid of literary or aesthetic qualities, but this was not always the case.

When written communication was first developed, literary narration and artistic renderings were merged with scientific and technical content. Cave paintings found in Alpera, France, dating back to 20,000 B.C., fuse narration and art to tell the story of various hunts. The fine lines and graceful curves depicting the small figure of the hunter against the two stags rising above him tell a story and provide instruction in one of the major occupations of that era.

The alphabet itself has evolved from a series of pictorial symbols known as logograms. Both the Semitic and Oriental alphabets began a little over 5,000 years ago in the form of pictographs, stylized pictures that symbolized objects. These were mainly used to record business transactions and transmit scientific and medical information. The Sumerians used pictographs to record inventories of various agricultural products. Tablets with cuneiform descriptions, an advanced form of pictography, were attached to sacks of grain and other products, indicating the quantity and type of produce inside the sacks. Sumerians also used pictographs, which preceded Egyptian hieroglyphics, to maintain records of pharmaceutical prescriptions and medical treatments as well as serve as literary chronicles.

The Chinese followed a similar pattern in their development of a written language. By the third century B.C., at the same time the Sumerians and Egyptians were involved with recording scientific and medical advances, the Chinese were writing books on pharmacology, alchemy, and medicine.

The fusion of art and the written word in technical documents continued through the Middle Ages, reaching its zenith in the illuminated manuscripts of the Irish monks. The style of these religious manuscripts, radiant with color and framing the texts in the dynamic lines and curves of abstract patterns, were carried into the Renaissance where they were used to decorate a large number of secular documents, including instructional manuals. Peele's *Pathewaye* (1569), an instructional manual on double-entry bookkeeping, uses the medieval convention of decorating the first letter in a chapter (cited in Tebeaux 1993), and Agricola's *De Re Metallica* (1950), a book on the art of metalworking, contains beautifully detailed and ornately decorated illustrations of the complex mechanisms used to mine precious ores (Figure 5–1).

Not only did art and text intertwine to create graceful, ornamental documents during the early period of written texts, but personal and business conventions blended to present messages in elegant and courteous prose. Letters for commercial purposes were written in a style that simulated a relationship akin to friendship, even when the correspondents were not close friends. In the second century A.D. Appolonius writes a letter to persuade Dioscurides to collect the accounts owed to him. Apollonius addresses his reader as his "very dear friend" though Dioscurides is only a business acquaintance. This personalization continues up through the Middle Ages. As late as the sixteenth century, Agricola was writing in the first person, often interjecting his own opinion into his discussions.

But following the medieval period, word and picture began to separate. Literary documents became increasingly text oriented, devoid of

Figure 5–1

A—Furnace. B—Its round hole. C—Air-holes. D—Mouth of the furnace. E—Draught opening under it. F—Earthenware crucible. G—Ampulla. H—Operculum. I—Its spout. K—Other ampulla. L—Basket in which this is usually placed lest it should be broken.

illustrations, and business and technical documents divested themselves of decorative elements, limiting visuals to charts and diagrams for practical purposes only. The Age of Reason was dominated by science and mathematics, verbal text, and arithmetic symbols; aesthetic and visual representation was usually considered irrelevant. A similar trend in which the elements of reason and emotion, aesthetics, and logic became separate entities occurred between personal and business prose. As individuals' public and private lives moved apart, texts became impersonal and lacked the graciousness of old.

Today, however, these trends appear to be reversing. Word and picture are merging once more, for both literary and technical documents, this time through the medium of the computer. Today we not only *read* the text of an article we have downloaded on our PC, but, by touching a highlighted hypertext word in the article, we can listen and watch a particular aspect of the topic in the form of a diagram or a narrated video which appears in an upper corner of our monitor. Home pages on the World Wide Web (WWW) testify to a return to decorative and personal texts, with their vast array of variegated and brilliant fonts and colorful, stylized clip art. PC menus appear against textured wall-papers. My laptop's icons appear over an artistic backdrop of Leonardo da Vinci's sketches of globes and air frames in muted violet tones. We can read our E-mail against colorful backgrounds. I like to send my notes in bright yellow text in contrast to a midnight blue background, the letters standing out like the moon on a clear night. I have a friend who prefers to use a drab khaki olive background; while another prefers a brilliant magenta text. In fact, color has become a dominant aspect of our communication culture; even our newspapers are splattered with color graphics. Software programs, such as Microsoft Office, allow us to write documents, incorporating charts and illustrations, and to decorate the pages with borders as ornate as those used by the monks of old.

As art and technology fuse today, so, too, are our personal lives fusing with the global community, fulfilling Pirsig's aspirations: "Technology is...a fusion of nature and the human spirit...that transcends them both. When this transcendence occurs, in such events as the first airplane flight across the ocean or the first footstep on the moon, a kind of public recognition of the transcendent nature of technology occurs. But this transcendence should also occur at the individual level, on a personal basis, in one's own life" (1976, 284–85). Through the computer, people are sending and receiving information related to their own personal lives, to the work in which they are engaged, and to solutions to global problems.

Olsen (1991) perceives visual representation as the most viable method for dealing with what appears to be insurmountable global problems. By organizing the overload of information flowing from government agencies and corporations through such visuals as graphs, tables, and maps, he believes computers will provide a means to make the data comprehensible to the human mind, allowing us to see complex relationships among a broad range of variables. Recognizing that even with the help of the computer, an interpretation of the visualized data still remains within the purview of the individual interpreting it, Hyerle warns that we need to be certain that our students become "skillful, reflective, mindful users of [visual] information" (1996, 16). We need to teach them how to read, interpret, evaluate, and apply the data as well as how to generate and discuss it.

This chapter is concerned with the merging of verbal, visual, textural, and multimedia elements that are increasingly comprising various forms of communication in the local and global workplace. We will look at these elements, examine how they are used, and consider methods for introducing them to our students. A concluding section suggests resources for learning about and acquiring the skills necessary for teaching students to use today's technology effectively and humanely.

Merging the Personal and Local
with the Social and Global

Guadalupe, Lupé (pronounced Yupé) for short, is a willowy Hispanic high school senior, with long, flowing black hair and large, brown eyes like the children in the sketches by Käthe Kollwitz. When she speaks, her voice is soft, tentative, and reticent. She seems more suited for a career in nursing or kindergarten teaching than in construction. Yet, she plans to enter the building trades.

Lupé became interested in the I.C.E. (Insulate Concrete Efficiently) Block Building System during a class in construction technology. The system was introduced recently into the United States to insulate buildings against extreme weather conditions, such as those found in Florida and Michigan. Lupé's teacher spent little time discussing the system, so when Lupé was assigned to write a report for her English class, she selected I.C.E. for her topic and set out to learn more about it. But she became stymied; a trip to the library did not turn up anything, and, worried that she might have to change her topic, she confided in one of her classmates. "Try the Internet," the classmate suggested. Five minutes later, Lupé had a list of recent sources that she could investigate. Ten minutes later she had copies of two recent and relevant articles and a catalog entry containing specifications for using the material. Lupé had used two search engines in Netscape, Acufind, and Alta Vista to locate her data.

Until this moment, the major source of knowledge for Lupé resided in books in a library. Now she had another source, the Internet, and this one, she learned, could provide current data and practical information on technical topics. From now on, it will be one of her primary sources, just as it has become a primary source for many people—students, workers, academicians, doctors, and lawyers.

In an article in the *Atlantic Monthly* (1994b), Michael Crichton, who portrays workers obtaining information in virtual cyberspace in his book, *Disclosure* (1994a), comments, "I especially want electronic searches. It is a continuous irony that as I am working on a novel, I can find any passage in it instantly with a keystroke, but at the same time I have heaps of books on my desk, on the floor, on the tables, and I must rummage through them like a rat looking for cheese to find some quote or note there" (15).

Communicating in an Increasingly Nonlinear, Sensory Environment

Not only are students and employees now obtaining information from a computer that they once obtained from a book, but they are receiving their information in a vastly different multimedia format. Often, it is not only textual, but visual, aural, textural, and kinesthetic. Graphics, illustrations, animation, videos, and audiotapes can be accessed for additional information about a topic. Simulations and interactive programs reinforce the information being presented by providing examples and virtual experiments.

These students are more visually literate and kinesthetically sensitive than their parents. They perceive and respond to a world in radically different ways than the baby boomers now reaching their half-century mark and preparing to retire from the workforce. Hyerle (1996) perceives teachers facing a new kind of student, who spends more time in front of a television or computer screen than in a classroom. Unlike the couch potatoes of the previous generation, who acquired little knowledge except that which related to soap operas and sitcoms, this generation is being overwhelmed with information: political information from CNN and other news networks, sports information from the sports network, historical information from the history network, science information from the science network, and literary information from the movie channels. We need to provide these students with tools to sift through all of this data, evaluate it, and synthesize that which is found relevant.

Anyone watching this generation of students manipulate a video game invariably recognizes that they can absorb and process far more sensory stimuli than those of previous generations. In terms of receiving and generating information, it appears that our students will prefer to obtain a large percentage of their knowledge from visual and aural media rather than printed documents, and that their presentation of information will tend to be visually and aurally based.

From watching disconnected scenes strung together in Sesame Street and video scenes, seemingly unconnected to the lyrics of the accompanying song, on MTV, this generation also has a far different perception of coherence and cohesion than their parents whose television program, *Laugh-in*, was the predecessor of this presentation form.

The consequences of these new perceptions are already evident. Today's students are as likely to acquire information in a nonlinear, branching type of search as they are in a linear, logical fashion. They are very comfortable following offshoots of a topic that may interest them, rather than keeping to a straight path. Thus, they're prior experience has prepared them for working in hypertext and multimedia environments.

Crichton (1994b) does not believe this desire for visual or aural information is limited to the new generation. He contends that even those of us over forty have wished for it, but we are all so accustomed to having only the printed text that we discount our wishes: "Certain subjects beg for multimedia and hypertext. I immediately think of art history and neuroanatomy....We are so accustomed to the inherent limitations of books that we do not hear the voice inside ourselves when we wish for more—when we read a text description and think, 'I wish I could see this painting he is talking about' or 'I wish I could see a diagram of this arrangement' or 'I wish I could hear the bird call he is describing'" (15).

Learning in an Increasingly Sensory Environment

Many students whose learning styles or intelligences are consonant with these new forms of communication will process the information they are acquiring much easier and better than they did when their only source was primarily textual (Peck and Dorricott 1994; Dwyer 1994). David Thornberg, author of *Edutrends 2010*, agrees. He comments: "If you create rich learning environments where multiple intelligences are addressed simultaneously, kids really thrive.... In making the classroom a more multisensory environment, you take advantage of these multiple pathways to learning.... Multimedia is a great tool because it combines images, text, animation—all sorts of sensory experiences (Betts 1994, 22).

Results of a two-year study by ACOT (Apple Classrooms of Tomorrow) of seven K–12 classrooms representing a cross section of American schools, support those of other studies (Boiarsky 1991): Students using computers wrote more, wrote more effectively, and had greater fluidity than students who didn't use computers (Dwyer 1994).

At an inner-city high school in San Diego, Linda Taggert (1994) moved beyond simple word processing to involve her students in the use of hypermedia. She found a "dramatic change" in her students: They are writing longer papers, spending more time revising, turning in better work, and enjoying what they are doing more, sometimes becoming so engrossed in a task that they don't hear the bell at the end of the period.

Mike Muir (1994) has seen a wide variety of changes in student behavior with the introduction of computers in his classroom in Maine. Reports written by special needs students compare favorably to those of others in the class. A student with behavioral problems becomes a patient peer tutor, "troublemakers" remain on-task and out of trouble, and "average" students become as involved as those designated "gifted."

Through using the computer, students not only enhance various aspects of their writing quality, enjoy creating, and become motivated to complete their tasks, but they also acquire content knowledge and other skills not usually associated with the study of English. ACOT found that students who used computers acquired many of the skills recommended in the SCANS report, including skills in collaborating, problem solving, and inquiring (Dwyer 1994).

Word processing, data bases, and graphic programs have made it possible for students to engage in large scale, authentic projects that require them to develop problem-solving strategies, learning to organize, analyze, interpret, develop, and evaluate their work (Peck and Dorricott 1994). Cliff Gilkey's project to develop multimedia curriculum materials on local Hispanic leaders in a rural area of California did just this. Gilkey wanted to provide his students with role models of leaders in their respective cultures—Hispanic, African American, and Vietnamese—but he couldn't find good materials for his students to read so he decided to get his students to write their own. Students researched and gathered information about local politicians, business people, researchers, and educators. Then they developed interview questions, and conducted and videotaped the interviews with the local leaders they had selected. Finally, they produced the materials. The class plans to sell the multimedia programs to schools in the region, and then use the money to help fund a science camp (Means and Olson 1994).

For a long time we bemoaned the fact that our classrooms cannot compete with television. Today, with the merging of computers and television, we can appropriate television as a powerful teaching tool. Similarly, we have bemoaned the decline in our students' reading. Today, they may be reading more than ever if we accept the computer monitor as a textual site. Epistolary discourse, which had all but disappeared, has been renewed with the introduction of E-mail. Writing, in fact, has increased, as our students chat and E-mail one another across geographic, racial, ethnic, and physical boundaries.

Integrating Computer Skills with Communication Strategies

Because audiences will increasingly prefer to receive information in a more sensory form than the traditional hard-copy text, and because

sensory forms of communication are already being used in the workplace, our students need to learn to communicate in these forms.
Thus, instruction in visual, aural, textural, and multimedia discourse
needs to become an integral aspect of the teaching of English.

We can no longer be concerned solely with written text or the traditional workplace genres of memos, letters, instructions, proposals,
and research reports. Students need to learn how to access the Internet, communicate via E-mail, create multimedia programs, and use
CDs for recording as well as playing. They also need to understand the
basic rubrics underlying word-processing programs, and be able to
apply these rubrics in order to use new versions of these programs. In
addition, they should be skilled in using databases, spreadsheets, and
graphics programs, as well as programs for presentations and desktop
publishing. Furthermore, they need to acquire skills for authoring
hypertext and multimedia programs.

The most opportune time to teach students the various applications is when they encounter a need to use them. A project-oriented
approach offers the best method for students to acquire computer literacy and become familiar with the way in which computers are used.
It is much easier for students to learn specific functions of a software
program that they can apply to a task immediately than general concepts for which they have no practical purpose at the time they are
learned. For example, asking students to conduct a survey and make
an oral presentation on the survey results can lead to students using
word processing, graphics presentation software, spreadsheets, and
desktop publishing tools, as it did in the following example.

At the school where I teach, the cafeteria doesn't remain open
after 6 PM, leaving evening students to snack out of machines in small,
crowded lounges. Our class decided to conduct a survey to learn if
enough students would eat at the cafeteria to make it profitable for the
eatery to remain open at night. Students used a word-processing program to develop the survey questionnaire. They then transferred the
document to a desktop publishing program, Pagemaker, in order to
have more control over the layout so that they could keep the survey
to a single, double-sided sheet of paper. In drafting their results, they
recognized that their readers would probably find it easier to understand the findings if the data were in table or graph form, so they used
a spreadsheet program, Excel, to chart their results. They then transferred the graphs to a presentation program, PowerPoint, for their oral
presentation. They also copied the headings and subheadings from
their reports onto slides in PowerPoint.

To provide this type of experience, students need access to a computer lab that contains all of the necessary software applications. They
also need enough time in the lab to work through a task and to feel

that they have accomplished their objective. For example, the class conducting the cafeteria survey needed to be able to create the layout for the survey in a single session, so that they could remember the different formats they had tried and the results of each trial. Rather than leaving the class frustrated that they had not yet found a way to keep the survey to a single page, the students needed to feel comfortable that they had arrived at a stopping place and were ready to go to the next task the following class. A single fifty-minute period is usually not sufficient. The new block system, using double class periods, gives students more time to work through a task, to collaborate and then work on their own, and to do the amount of revision necessary if a project is authentic.

In Canada, workplace English has been part of the curriculum for some time. Ron Blicq, a professional technical writer who has been working closely with the Canadian school system, recommends using "umbrella" projects which are very similar to the survey assignment discussed above. An umbrella project presents students with a problem and asks them to study it and then report on their findings. Because it requires fieldwork in gathering the information, and because the problem is usually a complex one, an umbrella project usually extends over several weeks. For example, Blicq suggests involving students in a study of sound levels in a school cafeteria or library:

> The students have to identify from whom to borrow a sound-level meter, write and telephone requests about it, research information on the effects of excessive sound, write and telephone to the owner or manager of the location where they will conduct their tests, write a trip report, progress report, and project completion report, and then document their findings and present their findings orally to their customer and to the remainder of the class. (Blicq 1994, 8–9)

Such a project offers a broad opportunity to use computer applications to engage in the various technological and communication tasks.

While students are learning various software applications, they should keep a notebook to jot down the various steps in which they engage for each task so that they can return to their notes when they need to repeat a task on the computer for another project. Acquiring skills in manipulating software applications is not like riding a bicycle; they are quickly forgotten if they aren't used frequently.

Furthermore, collaborative projects which involve pairing students to work on tasks can often reduce the amount of frustration students feel as they attempt to learn a software application. The "two heads are better than one" adage is relevant: When two people work on a single project, one can concentrate on working on the computer and using on-line help, while the other can scan the manuals for assistance.

Because many of these programs are site-licensed and there are not sufficient manuals for each student, you may want to purchase one of the software program texts that are on the market. Instructors here at Purdue Calumet have found that the Shelly Cashman series, published by International Thomson Publishing Company, provides a thorough, well-written, and user friendly series of textbooks for various programs that students find particularly helpful in learning a new program. The *Dummy* and *Dummy 101* series is less thorough, but is useful for providing easy-to-use instructions for a wide range of software programs.

Teaching Technology in an English Classroom

Technology in the classroom is a comparatively recent innovation. It has only been about ten years since computers were introduced into classes on a large scale basis. In many schools, that time is even shorter: the massive introduction of E-mail to communicate, of Internet as a means for gathering information, of the World Wide Web as a medium for graphics and hypertext, and of software programs, such as Microsoft Office, Pagemaker, Quark Express, Excel, PowerPoint, Acrobat, and Web Author for creating documents, presentations, and home pages has only come about in the last few years. For many of us, the attempt to keep apprised of what is occurring, let alone to acquire some competence in these new developments, is mind-boggling. And frightening. We seem to just acquire one set of competencies before we discover there are four more we need to master, each one appearing more complex than the one before it. Increasingly, we are expected to become technically skilled, yet most of us who are in English have had little interest in or innate aptitude for the technical. We are not like Pirsig's narrator; we have never combined our artistic inclinations with mechanical objects. Yet now we must do so if we are to prepare our students for the technological workplace of the twenty-first century.

We can no longer limit ourselves to teaching verbal text. Graphical, textural, and kinesthetic elements are already a part of the documents our students are reading, whether they are reading them in a hard-copy format or off a computer screen. If our students are to be prepared to enter the workplace, then we need to help them acquire skills in the various sensory modes.

Becoming Familiar with New Technology Software

We need to become familiar with the new technology and its applications, so we can serve as facilitators in helping our students acquire the skills necessary for using the technology in the workplace. To do so, we will need to attend workshops and seminars, read journals and manuals, and share our knowledge with our peers. It is a time-consuming endeavor, and, at the rate that new products are being introduced onto the market, it appears to be continual and never ending.

The best way to acquire a familiarity with the new technology and its applications is by attending workshops, seminars, or classes that offer hands-on training. Software companies not only sponsor such workshops, but many offer them free to educators with the hope that those attending will then order the programs for their schools. You may want to call various companies, such as Apple and Adobe Pagemaker, to find out if they offer such a series.

Colleges and universities also offer a variety of courses related to computers. Those that are the most relevant will probably be offered by English Departments and will be related to business and technical writing. Some universities offer specific courses in desktop publishing, and writing in multimedia and hypertext.

Although the best way to learn about the various applications is through hands-on experience, articles in professional journals can provide suggestions for using the software programs in the classroom, as well as keep you abreast of the latest trends. During the past year, several textbooks have come on the market which can help you provide students with a basic understanding of the technology. *The Online Student* by Reddick and King (1996) is one of the best in this line.

While we may acquire some rudimentary skills in these programs, most of us will not become experts. We have neither the time nor the motivation to do so. Instead, we need to find alternative ways to provide our students with the instruction they need. One place we can turn is to the students themselves. Usually in any class, there are several students who are quite knowledgeable about the programs we want to introduce. We can also turn to the experts, those who teach computer skills, to offer the kinds of courses we are suggesting as part of the school's curriculum. We might also collaborate with other members of our school's faculty. Some of us are already knowledgeable in using the Internet or in creating Web pages, while others are competent in using PowerPoint and graphics programs. Through forward-looking scheduling and carefully planned projects, we can engage in team teaching the various aspects of computers that students need to learn. Team teaching not only provides students with instruction from the most qualified person in a specific area, but it also gives us an opportunity to learn from our colleagues.

By moving gracefully into the twenty-first century and adopting the best that it has to offer, we can transform our classrooms to enhance our teaching. Our classrooms will actually be easier to conduct because our students will be learning to process and manipulate the kinds of sensory data from which they themselves learn best, and they will be learning to use these elements in the kind of hands-on, collaborative, authentic, project-oriented environment in which they thrive.

The remainder of this chapter discusses a variety of computer applications that students will need to know in the workplace, and offers suggestions for projects to familiarize them with these applications. A final section offers recommendations for becoming current and staying on top of the technologies students will need to use to communicate in the twenty-first century.

Computer Environments and Applications

The two major computer environments are those of Apple and Windows, and these are slowly merging. Because most businesses use Windows, students need to become familiar with this environment. They need to understand how the desktop works, how color and texture are manipulated to provide various backgrounds and texts, and how applications software is used.

The Desktop

One of the first projects you may want to assign is that of setting up the desktop for personal preference. This will give students the opportunity to play with various aspects of the computer as well as become acquainted with their desktop. They can learn to change the color and texture of their screen, to alter the wallpaper on their screen saver, and to manipulate the color of the background and text in the various programs on their desktop.

Word Processing, Databases, and Templates

Because letters and memoranda should be kept short, not more than a single page, and because the content can be fairly simple, a good time to introduce students to word processing is during a unit on correspondence. By using the templates provided by the various word-processing programs, students can easily create correspondence that conforms to the conventions for the various subgenres.

A unit on letters and memoranda also provides a good opportunity for teaching students to set up and use databases for maintaining mailing lists. Databases allow students to personalize form letters and to create address labels through the mail merge function. (Simplified versions of databases are often included in word-processing programs.) Students might be assigned to write a memorandum to remind teachers of an upcoming PTA meeting. To fulfill the assignment, students need to create a database of the school's faculty that includes names, addresses, and phone numbers for each teacher. By using the database, they can personalize the memo and create labels for the envelopes in which the memo is to be sent.

Presentation and Graphics Software

In Chapter 2, I discussed that, regardless of the position employees hold, they may be required to make extemporaneous, informal presentations, and I indicated that presentations are more effective when accompanied by visuals. The computer can be used both to create and present these visuals. Presentation programs, such as PowerPoint, simplify the process of creating slides or overhead transparencies, by providing templates, background patterns, palettes of color, and clip art, from which students can select those that are appropriate for their purpose and audience. These programs also possess capabilities for dissolving and sequencing slides during a presentation. The presenter has the option of printing out colored transparencies or of projecting a slide show directly from a computer, using an LCD projector. (An LCD projector allows a presenter to project the screen of a computer onto a large movie screen, so the audience can see what is happening as the presenter manipulates the computer.)

Because these programs involve visual and kinesthetic approaches to processing information, they reflect the learning styles of many business and technical students. I have found that students who might otherwise procrastinate or fail to draft a report are often motivated to work on such projects, and that their presentations are often very good. For this reason, when I assign a major report, I also require students to make an oral presentation on the same topic. I have found that as students become involved in creating the transparencies for their visual presentation, they become more organized in categorizing their information into related chunks, and consequently revise their written reports. Thus, their visual drafts inform their verbal texts.

During this unit I have an opportunity to introduce students to spreadsheet programs so that they learn to use the computer to work with numerical data. Excel and graphics programs, such as Harvard Graphics, are capable of converting numerical data into graphic forms, such as tables, bar, and pie charts. To transform the numerical data into appropriate graphic form, students need to analyze, synthesize, and evaluate it, thus engaging in higher-level cognitive skills. The Caterpillar quality team's evaluation report for the paint line for the D-6 Tractor includes numerous charts that the writers created to provide readers with a visual picture of their section's improvements. A lesson in creating graphics and charts easily lends itself to team teaching with someone from the mathematics department who might review percentages, fractions, and estimation with students.

I prefer real-life situations rather than casebook scenarios for these assignments so that students have real audiences with real purposes to whom they are making their presentations and presenting their reports. For example, I recently assigned students to conduct a needs assessment for the Career Development and Placement Office (CD&P) in an effort to find ways to increase students' use of CD&P. After my class had listened to an explanation of the CD&P Office by a member of the staff, I divided the students into groups, with each group assigned several specific tasks. One group examined the computer services being offered, another group evaluated a CD&P-sponsored workshop, a third group studied the office's public relations strategies and documents, and the entire class analyzed the responses to a survey. A member of one of the groups even tested the response of the office staff to student drop-ins. Halfway through the project, each student was required to write a progress report. At the end of the project, each student wrote an observation and evaluation report for the specific task in which they were involved. Each group then synthesized the information in the individual reports, and prepared a group report and oral presentation on their assessment results.

When each group's portion of the written report was complete, their drafts were duplicated and distributed to all members of the class. Groups were then variously assigned to write the cover page, table of contents, executive summary, introduction, and procedures sections of the report. Each section was then combined into a single class report by a group of students who had volunteered to serve as the editorial staff. A different editorial group placed all of the slides for the oral presentation into a single computer file.

A representative from the CD&P Office was invited to the class to hear the presentation. Various members of each group delivered their portion of the report. Afterward, the representative was given a copy of the written report. A question and answer session between the representative and the class ensued.

The unit was approximately eight weeks. During this period, students learned the following skills:

- writing a progress report
- writing an evaluation report
- writing an observation report
- writing a needs assessment report

- editing a collaborative report
- writing about numbers
- evaluating a survey questionnaire
- interpreting the results of a survey
- drafting an oral presentation
- creating graphics to visually display the survey's numerical results
- creating a slide presentation
- importing graphics from one software program into another
- using clip art, color, and background textures
- collaborating on a project
- arriving at consensus
- problem solving

How well did they learn them? Since taking my class, Greta has assumed the role of faculty consultant. Whenever she's in a classroom or attending a lecture in which the transparencies are illegible, she offers to train the teacher in using PowerPoint to make better visuals. Our students can quickly become our teachers in this field.

Desktop Publishing

Occasionally employees are needed to edit newsletters, or prepare brochures and announcements regarding an activity in which their division or team is involved. Bob Webb, an hourly worker, became a member of the Communication Committee at John Deere, where he wrote articles for an employee newsletter while Lori Wedland, a right-of-way agent, helped gather information for a "Random Acts of Kindness" column in the Cilco newsletter.

If employees also have desktop publishing skills, they can often assume a leadership position in an activity. Word-processing programs, such as Microsoft Word, usually have desktop publishing capabilities built in, but the functions they can perform are often limited. However, programs that are specifically designated as desktop publishing, such as Pagemaker and Quark Express, have a broad range of capabilities and, if possible, students should have opportunities to work on these. In teaching desktop publishing, you will need to provide instruction in page and screen layout, type face and size, borders and backgrounds, and graphics, including charts, illustrations, and clip art.

At Brimfield High School in Illinois, Jim Blane conducts a desktop publishing class, using CorelOffice. Jim solicits jobs from the business community for the students to do. The class publishes the school district's monthly newsletter. In addition, his classes have designed doorknob hangers for a local insurance company, published the phone directory for the local hockey league, and created direct-mail coupons for a local restaurant. The payment the class receives for these jobs is used to purchase upgrades in both hardware and software. Thus, Jim's students learn to use a variety of software programs, while they are simultaneously learning to write, design, and publish brochures, advertisements, business cards, and announcements that are of professional quality. States one student, "Everything has to be done to perfection. Nothing can be done wrong for a customer." In other words, C work doesn't cut it. Says Blane, "To get paid for the job, they have to complete it exactly the way the customer wants it" (Gagon 1995).

Many students enjoy desktop publishing because it allows them to be visually creative: "These tools provide forms of artistic communication for those students who have been constrained by the traditional options of verbal and written communication, and they increase motivation and foster creative problem-solving skills, as students evaluate the many possible ways to communicate ideas" (Peck and Dorricott 1994).

Sharon Strenth uses the following activity in her English class.

Research and Travel Brochure for World History Lesson

Approach:

- Teaching to formulate questions (to think) before beginning research
- Teaching steps in process writing
- Designing a travel brochure with audience and purpose in mind

Objectives:

- Students will prewrite about a vacation.
- Students will study travel brochures for content (print, graphics, visual appeal).
- Students will transfer features from model brochures to their own assignment.
- Students will consider audience and purpose.
- Students will prioritize features they wish to include in their brochures.
- Students will generate specific questions they need authoritative answers to in order to publish their work.

Activity:

1. Students journal write about *vacation.*

2. Students compile lists of features they discover in the travel brochures provided (small group).

3. Students become members of Louis XIV's (The Sun King) Department of Tourism, and are charged with the responsibility of creating a promotional brochure for the Palace of Versailles. They are told that tourism is a crucial business, since Louis has nearly depleted the country's once-rich treasury. They hope to attract French countrymen as well as people all over the globe to this magnificent palace.

4. Students compile a list of questions they need to have answered before they can complete such an assignment. Each group's list is shared with the entire class (small group).

5. Students suggest what other tasks need to be completed before their project can be completed (small group and then entire class).

E-Mail

Students need to learn the conventions associated with E-mail, such as those related to addressing and signing a message. A set of conventions called *netiquette* has also developed around this form of communication. Netiquette is the Martha Stewart version of etiquette on the Internet. It includes such dos and don'ts as "Don't scream (type in all caps)," "If you join a discussion group, introduce yourself briefly when you enter," "Refrain from flaming (expressing how you feel about a person or topic in all-out, no-holds-barred terms)," and, "Convey your emotions with emoticons (i.e., if you're being sarcastic or trying to be funny, follow your remark with a smiley face so the audience knows what you're up to and doesn't misinterpret your message)" (Rubin 1994).

Once students have been introduced to E-mail, they should be given opportunities to practice using it. This is usually easy to accomplish. Students seem to find corresponding socially with one another via E-mail as enjoyable as passing notes. If they are working in groups, they can use E-mail to communicate with one another. When they engage in a project, they can use E-mail to communicate with you concerning questions they may have about their work.

There are also a number of opportunities for students to use E-mail nationally and internationally, for both social and academic purposes. One student commented how her E-mail friends in Australia, Slovenia, and Argentina helped her understand people from across the world (Educational Research Service [ERS] 1995). Several networks are set up that help students find pen pals around the globe. In addition, there are networks that provide opportunities for students to share information about specific subjects. For example, classes around the world can collaborate on a project related to one of six subject areas provided by the AT&T Learning Network. These include language, creative writing, places and perspectives around the country, energy, society's problems, and global issues. Students research and exchange information with one another. When a group of students decided to learn about the Berlin Wall, they didn't just use books; they sent a list of questions to the members of their circle in Berlin. World Classroom is another such network that provides access to people around the globe. Not only do students become accustomed to using this form of communication, but they also gain knowledge about various cultures and nations on every continent, knowledge that has become increasingly necessary for working effectively in our global economy.

E-mail can be used in conjunction with units in literature as well as content areas. *Listservs* can be used for discussions about books students are reading. They can exchange ideas about a book with students who have read the same book regardless of whether they are in the same class or across the country. In addition, living authors sometimes have E-mail addresses where students can write to ask them about their works.

Regardless of the purpose, by using E-mail, students are becoming familiar with its conventions and comfortable with it as a form of communication.

Internet

All over the country, students, like Lupé, are gathering information for reports and proposals via the Information Superhighway. Minnesota students have tracked the movement of the seasons across the country by asking students in other states to send in signs of spring as they appear. Students in Maryland are participating in a NASA scientific satellite mission, collecting actual data and monitoring systems, and students in Virginia are comparing environments and cultures with students around the world. According to the Educational Research Service (ERS), students are using the Internet for news retrieval, weather information, scientific databases, and encyclopedia searches (cited in School Board News 1995.)

Students need to become as accustomed to using on-line searches to obtain information as they have become used to going to a library. And just as they need to learn the Dewey decimal system in order to locate a book they want, they need to understand how to locate appropriate on-line sources, navigate through them, become familiar with the kinds of data they provide, and finally use, cite, and reference the data they obtain. Patricia LeRoy (1991), who teaches at Cassville High School in Wisconsin, requires that her students use on-line searches to obtain information for the topics they select for their research papers. Students run a search and then use the printout to order copies of the information they want. She has found that the excitement elicited when the information arrives serves to motivate the students to read the material as soon as they receive it.

We need to provide students with opportunities to access the Internet and help them learn to navigate its highways by creating projects that encourage them to acquire information from it. In addition to using library resources, students should be encouraged to search the Internet for information about the topics they are writing research papers on, or on subjects they become interested in because they discover them in books they are reading. Eileen Schwartz of Purdue University Calumet developed a partial list of Internet sources that teachers and students can use for various research projects:

Suggested Web Sites for Workplace English

Business Sources—explains how to start a business

Simitel Software Repository—programs and utilities for a myriad of subject areas

Paramind—brainstorm tool to help get ideas focused

KIDLINK (ages 10–15)—a global dialog link to 30,000 children in sixty-seven countries

NCRS (Natural Resources Conservation Service)—links to government agencies on conserving soil, air, water, plants

Internet Movie Database (AKA Cardiff's Movie Database Browser)—movie reviews, news, excellent source of movie information

Literature and Writing Resources—on-line texts, critical texts, literary journals, writers' resources

Galaxy World—information on cities and countries worldwide

American Memory—on-line photographs, films, documents, and recordings of American History and Culture

FedWorld—government documents with access to approximately 140 agencies

PolicyNet—public policy issues

NARA (National Archives and Records Administration)—clearing-house of information on presidential libraries

THOMAS—information on federal legislation; house and senate bills and congressional record

Academy One—a variety of projects for students in a variety of areas, i.e., space simulation, bird migration, etc.

WEBB66—provides web links to schools around the world; help in establishing Internet services and funding K–12 resources, lesson plans for teachers, projects for students, even tutors

NOW (National Organization for Women)—information on various issues, i.e., social welfare, national defense, etc.

Lessons related to literature can also involve the Internet, thereby providing students with expanded opportunities to become acquainted with the kinds of information databases available. Students can use the Web to locate critical analyses of the literary works they're reading, biographies of the authors, various manuscript versions, visual presentations of the settings in which a literary work takes place, and sometimes even movie versions of the work.

Kelly Jackson Kennedy has developed the following lesson to accompany students' reading of *Animal Farm* in her classroom in Ladson, South Carolina.

Activity

Directions: A common barrier in communication occurs when the sender takes for granted the fact that the receiver has the same knowledge base. This may occur when one reads *Animal Farm* by George Orwell because the characters and events in the book represent people and events which occurred before and during Orwell's lifetime. Because of this, he can create characters and plots which relate to them. However, the reader may not have the same knowledge base; therefore, he may not understand the "fairy story" completely. To avoid this, we are going to research characters and events which served as the models for the story.

Using the World Book Information Finder on your computer, find information about the following people and events:

Socialism	Capitalism
Karl Marx	Napoleon
Czar Nicholas II	Leon Trotsky

Joseph Stalin   V.I. Lenin

Bolshevik Revolution   Bourgeoisie

Proletariat   Secret Police (KGB)

Use of propaganda to control minds

After you read the book, discuss the similarities between the characters and events in the book with those in history. You may do this in chart form if you wish.

The information that can be obtained from the World Wide Web and the other data bases extends far beyond the impersonal data required for an academic or business report. People can also access information that is related to their personal lives. Students who are considering some form of education beyond high school can study the catalogs and brochures of many of the institutions over the Internet. One site, College Town, offers a virtual tour of over 750 colleges and universities, with information on scholarships and loans included. In addition, the site has links to athletic recruiters and provides opportunities to send messages directly to the respective admissions offices. The Internet College Exchange provides addresses and phone numbers to over 5,000 institutions of higher education, while Black Excel provides a guide to historically black institutions (Sheppard 1996).

Increasingly, businesses are posting job openings and requesting that resumes be sent over the net. Many of these openings are listed with on-line headhunters, such as Job Bank USA or the National Resume Bank (Hanson 1996). Civil service jobs are routinely listed. Internships are also being posted. A student at Purdue University Calumet in Indiana spotted a posting for an internship in technical writing with IBM in Minnesota. She sent in her application via E-mail and was accepted. We need to provide students with help in writing resumes and letters of application for the Internet. To understand requirements for formatting a document that is going to be transmitted via the Internet, students need to learn how information is transmitted on-line as well as the conventions for on-line documents. They need to recognize that simple formats with common fonts rather than unique formats are the best way to send documents on-line because the receiving computer may not have some of the fancier fonts or be able to translate a complex format.

Netscape has become a common term and almost everyone, it seems, is creating a Web site. Car salesmen advertise their cars, colleges advertise their academic offerings, and people advertise everything from their marital availability to their desire to take a trip to Bermuda. Companies are paying agencies large sums of money to create unique home pages, recognizing that this is the first screen that everyone sees. The home page is the hook, the motivating factor that entices visitors to go further into a site. Screens are often glitzy, colorful, playful, and animated.

Students not only need to become familiar with the contents on the Web and with navigating its colorful corridors, but they need to learn to create their own sites. A variety of software programs provide authoring tools that enable students to develop pages for a site that includes graphics, multimedia, and hypertext. You may want to create a school or class site in which each student can incorporate his or her own page. For example, Linda Taggert (1994), who teaches at the San Diego Memorial Academy for International Baccalaureate Preparation, has integrated her traditional unit on autobiographical writing with the teaching of hypertext. The result is an "electronic flip book," in which students record their histories along with pictures of important events and people in their lives. These could have been transferred to a class Web site. In a variation on a theme, Catherine Morics (1991), who teaches at Greenfield High School in Greenfield, Wisconsin, and James Ross (1991), who teaches at Webster Traditional School in Cedarburg, Wisconsin, create autobiographical newspapers. It is a small step to placing these on hypercards and then organizing them to create a class Web site.

Multimedia and Hypermedia

Multimedia is not a new phenomenon. The mixing of film and slides to create multi-image presentations became a prominent audiovisual form in the 1970s. The multimax screens seen mainly at such places as the Franklin Institute in Philadelphia, the Museum of Science and Industry in Chicago, and the Air and Space Museum in Washington, D.C., use this form of presentation. Students can also use multimedia as an alternative form for presenting information. Instead of a written research report as the end product of a unit, students might be assigned to create a multimedia presentation. In Columbus, Ohio, one group of students produced a video disc showing a scale model of the city's renovated business district.

While multimedia may be an old medium, it has been given a new twist with the introduction of hypermedia. Hypermedia is the presentation of various elements of multimedia in a hypertext (multilayered text) environment. In other words, a document might contain text, slides, animation, video, voice, and music, all easily accessible at the click of a mouse. A report on nuclear waste may contain data about the amount of waste in existence, photographs showing where the waste is presently stored, tables listing the amount of waste at each site, animation explaining where the waste comes from, and videos following the waste as it is transported across the country. The audio might include a narrator's voice as well as the voices of several officials from the Nuclear Regulatory Commission. An increasing number of programs are available which incorporate hypermedia, and people are beginning to use hypermedia in their Web pages. Once students learn to use hypertext, it is a small step for them to acquire skills to integrate multimedia into their documents. While in many cases students can find visuals already available to import into their hypermedia documents, they may increasingly recognize the need to develop their own. The need to use either animation or video offers an opportunity to provide students instruction in film making and scripting, a skill the members of the quality team at Caterpillar needed to acquire in order to produce the training film for their paint line.

Just as students need to develop schema for workplace documents, such as proposals and evaluation reports, in order to write them effectively, they need to develop schema for multimedia and hypertext documents and presentations in order to create them successfully. Likewise, just as they develop schema for workplace documents by reading them, they can develop schema for technologically based documents by experiencing them. Therefore, we need to provide students with opportunities to experience a wide variety of multimedia and hypertext documents and presentations, such as *Alice to Ocean* and the IBM Greek mythology series, *Ulysses.*

We can find many of these documents on the Web. You might want to add Web home pages to a unit on advertising, asking students to analyze and review multimedia and hypertext presentations in light of what they know about good advertising techniques. In addition to the Web, students can view a large number of multimedia programs, such as the *Virtual Biopark* or *Amazonia* by Computer Curriculum Corporation, in their content courses. You may want to encourage faculty in science or technology to show these programs in their classes.

Some programs are also being developed for literature. The electronic arm of Penguin Press has just completed a hypermedia version of John Steinbeck's *Of Mice and Men.* The cyberversion mixes text with music, clips from the 1992 John Malkovic and Gary Sinise film version, historical photographs from Steinbeck's youth in California, personal letters, souvenirs, and mementos of the author, and anecdotes from the author's widow, Elaine Steinbeck (Leyva 1996).

Conclusion

Text, texture, word, and picture all fuse in today's communication documents. Documents move with animated videos, ideas are voiced, and personal thoughts travel in convoluted circles, communicating with hundreds, or even thousands, on every continent. The teaching of English extends far beyond the traditional texts of Shakespeare and Milton and the manual forms of composing with pen and paper or typewriter. It encompasses visual, textural, and kinesthetic documents as well as textual ones, all produced technologically, to fuse "nature and the human spirit into a new kind of creation that transcends both" (Pirsig 1976, 284).

English is in the process of becoming a new field, fraught with challenges but overflowing with creative energy. By transmitting that energy to our students, we can empower them to engage fully in the social, political, economic, and aesthetic moments of their lives.

Six

Collaboration and Integration in Workplace English

At six-foot-four, Alan Spanjer towers above my five-foot frame. When I was at Georgia State University, he and I shared an office where we spent many long hours collaborating on articles and on coordinating the Georgia State University Writing Project. Allan was a specialist in curriculum development, having spent time at the Educational Laboratory in Oregon, while I came out of a writing background and had had a stint with United Press International. Periodically, Alan would toss a manuscript onto my desk and ask me to look it over. Then he would pace back and forth, waiting for my reaction. In that typical four-by-four faculty office, he'd manage to take about four paces before he'd have to turn around and go back the other way. When I'd come to a section in the draft that wasn't clear, he'd stop pacing and try to explain what he meant, stroking his graying beard as if it held the secret and had only to be caressed to give forth a clear message, like a bottle with a genie inside. Sometimes it took two or three tries before I understood what Alan was trying to say. When I did, I would cross out the problem section and write in a new statement, based on the notes I'd taken as he paced.

At other times, Alan and I would sit side by side at his desk, trying to revise my plans for a curriculum for our Writing Project. I didn't know much about sequencing a curriculum then, so Alan explained the various theories and concepts, such as learning development and the teachable moment, that inform curriculum planning.

It was a good collaboration. I learned about curriculum development from Alan. He learned about writing from me.

I've had other collaborative arrangements that worked out well. Many of these related to projects I worked on, rather than manuscripts. I learned about nuclear utilities from a colleague from Georgia Tech, Leah McNeill, while I taught her about the writing process. She and I spent hours sipping wine, arguing over the relationship of Flower's model of composing to the documents written at the nuclear utility where we were conducting workshops in effective writing. Through our sometimes heated collaboration, we were able to develop training programs that successfully solved our clients' problems.

And here at Purdue Calumet, Eileen Schwartz and I share ideas about the teachers and programs for our Writing Project over the telephone, across the lunch table, and in the car as we travel to various schools in our area. Eileen knows the region and the politics of the local public schools, and, as a newcomer to this region, I listen intently to what she has to say. I teach her about the Writing Project.

Collaboration. It alleviates the isolation. It enables us to create, develop, and produce the kinds of manuscripts, theories, and projects that we cannot develop by ourselves. It opens doors so ideas can be exchanged; it expands our knowledge; it enhances our projects. It allows us to create a community of teacher/writers who care about the quality of their work and about the lives of the students they teach.

From Isolation to Collaboration

Collaboration has run as a leitmotif through the pedagogical literature of the past decade. We have introduced group work into our classrooms, teaming students to prewrite, to peer conference, to respond to their reading, and to engage in project work. Moffett and Wagner (1992) extol the benefits of interaction for its value to both "exploit individual variation" and to "pool social resources....Pooling knowledge,...stimulating and supporting each other, using each other as audience—these are all practical ways to give individuals the advantage of numbers. Internalizing, feeding back, and comparing mental sets go deeper. They are three major learning methods" (34).

But despite our convictions that engaging our students in collaborative activities will provide them with support for acquiring a wide variety of language arts and social skills, we do comparatively little collaboration ourselves. Although increasingly we work in committees, we usually sigh with relief when the committees adjourn, anxious to get back to whatever tasks (or papers) we have left behind.

All too often, we return to our classrooms, close our doors, and implement the committees' decisions in isolation. And it is in isolation that we grapple with the problems of students who don't turn in assignments because they are holding down a job to help support their family, whose writing appears incoherent, whose reading skills are far below grade level, or who cannot become literate in terms of the Internet because they don't have a telephone in their homes. It is in isolation that we try to keep up with the latest computer software, with the most recent pedagogical trends, and with the newest research findings related to the brain. And it is in isolation that we attempt to write new lesson plans for a workplace English curriculum. In most cases, these tasks can be lightened and the problems handled more effectively if we would leave the isolation of our classrooms for a congenial gathering place, where we could meet in a collaborative effort to destroy the barriers that hinder students from learning. According to Kagan (1989/90), "Cooperative...methods are very powerful: they allow us to reach our objectives more efficiently" (10). Sharan and Sharan (1989/90) agree: "[By] cooperating..., [the members of the group] can achieve more than they would as individuals. The final result of the group's work reflects each member's contribution, but it is intellectually richer than work done individually" (17).

The positive gains in knowledge, skills, and social and cultural growth that our students make in participating in collaborative activities can also be made by us (Greene 1991). We, too, can engage more successfully in problem solving if we become part of a collaborative effort. DiPardo (1996) describes the effect of teamwork on two teachers, Bill, an English teacher, and Max, a computer whiz, who team teach a course in magazine writing and editing at a small alternative school. They collaborate on a daily basis to try to solve the minute-to-minute challenges that face them in a classroom filled with students in trouble with the law, with bright blue Mohawks, with pro-marijuana T-shirts, with learning disabilities, and with kids of their own. Their type of collaboration, "born of mutual concern for students, a shared search for better strategies and solutions, and a wise willingness to wonder and wait," may not have always "lightened the load, [but] at least it helped them better understand the nature of all they were up against" (123).

Not only do we need to collaborate among ourselves, but we need to extend our boundaries and collaborate with our community at large. This must take place if we are to effectively solve many of the challenges facing us in the classroom, since many of the problems that affect students' learning are caused by forces outside the school, such as pregnancy, poor health and nutrition, drugs, and parental neglect or abuse. Project Success, a pilot program sponsored by the North Central Regional Educational Laboratory (NCREL), found that when education, health, and social service agencies work together, student problems can often be solved easily and quickly (NCREL 1994). For example, by meeting with health and social service officials to discuss how a student with acute menstrual pain could receive medical assistance, school officials were able to solve the problem of the student's high absentee rate at her high school.

In these collaborative efforts, not only do we gain in knowledge and perhaps wisdom, but our students gain also. Recent research indicates that "Isolated teachers are less successful than their collaborative counterparts" (DiPardo 1996, 109). Rosenholtz (1985) found that students learn more effectively in courses in which they are asked to engage in problem solving that involves multiple disciplines. These are courses that can only be effective if the teachers of the various disciplines have collaborated to design problem-solving activities, and to pool their resources for instructional purposes.

What Is Collaboration?

Collaboration can be defined in a variety of ways: Judith Warren Little (1990) defines collaboration as "joint work—interdependent professional activity involving conscious structuring of time and task, as well as teacher leadership and initiative" (519). The key word here is *interdependent:* A project cannot be carried out without each person's participation in the project.

Collaboration can assume a variety of forms, including parallel and intersecting. In parallel collaboration, each group member works for a common goal but does so independently (Levak, Merryfield, and Wilson 1993). For example, a faculty at a school may select a common theme, "Labor in the Industrial World," around which all of the faculty teach. Classes examine the theme from the perspective of their own disciplines, using their own lesson plans and activities. The social studies class may study the history of labor unions, the math class may look at union trends, biology classes may study agricultural unions, the various vocational classes may learn about the unions in their respective areas, and English classes may read Dickens' *Hard Times* and Hailey's *Wheels* and watch the film *Norma Rae.*

In intersecting collaboration, disciplines are interwoven. For example, for that same theme, students may be given a scenario in which a local union wants to develop a packet of materials to encourage new employees at a plant to join the organization. Students need to incorporate the information they obtain from each of the various disciplines into the packet. To initiate this kind of project requires that teachers attend meetings throughout the project, as they report to each other where they are in their lessons and what pieces of infomation they need from each other in order for their students to meet the final deadline with a complete package of materials.

Collaborating to Integrate the Curriculum

Collaboration and integration go hand in hand when we talk about language learning, literacy, and the workplace. Through collaborative activities, students can communicate about their vocational fields. Dyson (1989) writes: "Throughout the history of American schooling, educators have periodically called for the integration of the language arts—for writing, reading, talking, and listening to become collaborative processes in classroom activities, thereby furthering the development of each process and, more importantly, furthering children's learning about themselves and their world" (3).

Traditionally, teaching has been a fragmented experience. We attempt to teach students self-contained, fifty-minute lessons that not only cover the contents of an 800-page anthology, but include the requirements mandated by the state and whatever additional information we believe they need to know. As we have been required to impart more and more pieces of discrete information to more and more students with more and more learning problems, we have increasingly recognized the futility of our task. We are not only burning ourselves out, but we are also driving our students out (Jacobs 1989). Of necessity, we need to find a better way to provide our students with the knowledge and skills they need. We can, of course, look at our English curriculum and prune it. But to do that, we need to decide exactly what it is we wish to teach. If we wish to teach both content and procedural knowledge, and if we recognize the need to incorporate workplace English into the curriculum, then we will need to prune the traditional curriculum almost down to the roots. In so doing, we could kill the whole bush. Instead, we need to search for a better way to achieve our goals by examining the curriculum, not just in English, but in all of the disciplines being offered. Such an examination should reveal what many of us have suspected—a great deal of overlap exists. We will likely find that the history department is teaching themes that relate to the novels we are teaching in the English department; the biology department is assigning readings related to the environment that are similar to those included in the anthologies used by English classes; and the lessons in a math class concerned with converting numbers to percentages relate to the lessons in an English class that revolve around teaching students to conduct surveys and report on the results.

By integrating the overlapping aspects of these courses, we can provide students with a more holistic view of the knowledge they're learning. We can also provide them with the "how tos" for working within their vocational fields. Ackerman and Perkins (1989) emphasize the importance of integrating declarative and procedural knowledge "because the 'skills' may be helpful, even essential, to students trying to unlock the content" (79). For example, the readings for both a biology and an English class could be identical, but the focus of each class could differ. The English class could focus on procedural knowledge, i.e., the aspects of an article that cause it to be a good example of scientific writing, while the biology class could focus on content knowledge.

This idea is extended by Caine and Caine (1991), when they write "Integration, by reducing duplication of both skills and content, begins to allow us to teach more. It also gives us a new perspective on what constitutes basic skills,...[It] connects subject areas that reflect the real world" (119). But integrating the curriculum makes sense on a cognitive level as well as for administrative purposes. Recent brain research indicates that the brain searches for patterns and interconnections as its way of making meaning. Not only does it allow us to teach more by eliminating duplication, but it allows our students, especially those who are experiential learners, to learn better. It provides a means for engaging them in authentic activities because they are reading and writing to do something in a real-world context—even if that world has been constructed by their vocational course. Writing a progress report about their progress on a project in their graphic design course is far more authentic than writing an essay for English class on the need for a cushion for social welfare mothers. Furthermore, an integrated curriculum is consistent with what we know of learning patterns. Rather than acquiring discrete bits of unconnected data, an integrated curriculum builds on the relationships that exist among pieces of data and between prior knowledge and new information, allowing our students to make connections that build into learned concepts that are retained longer than isolated facts (Katz 1985).

If we are to institute an effective workplace English curriculum in our schools, then we need to integrate the various segments of the language arts—reading, writing, listening, speaking, and visualizing—with computer programs, various other academic areas, vocational areas, and with the workplace itself. To create such an integrated curriculum, we need to engage in collaborative activities with a broad range of people—with our students, other members of our department, faculty members in other departments, and with business, industry, and community members. In the remainder of this chapter we will discuss how we can collaborate with our students, with other faculty members, and with members of the community.

Collaborating with Our Students

In the previous chapter, we suggested a collaboration with our students in relation to teaching computer application programs. Allowing students to become peer tutors in our computer labs frees us to do what we are most knowledgeable in—teaching our students how to write and design the documents that these computer programs make possible.

But it is not just in relation to computers that our students are more knowledgeable than we are. Those students whose interests lie in technology have acquired a great deal more knowledge and skills related to construction, electronics, mechanics, biology, and the justice system than most of us who teach English. Not only do we need to collaborate with our students in teaching various computer applications, but we need to collaborate with them in teaching workplace English, giving them the opportunity to use their technological expertise as the content of their documents. This form of collaboration allows us to help them learn to write and it allows them to provide us with information about the technological world in which they work. For example, one of my students, Ben Acheff, had written a report on digital imaging. Portions of his report had been unclear, and I had met with him to get a better explanation. As an old devotee of black-and-white photography, I was fascinated with the topic. Ben, a tall, thin kid with rapid-fire speech and movements that matched the staccato sounds of the Nintendo, clarified most of the points on which I was confused, and in so doing enabled me to suggest ways he could revise his report so that it would be clear for other readers. Anxious to make the changes, he had another draft for me by the end of the period. Ben and I had collaborated. In addition, my interest in his topic had created an atmosphere that enabled me to make suggestions without his feeling defensive. My interest had elicited the information from him that clarified the points in his report. In response, his explanations had helped me understand the topic. My interest had also motivated him to make the necessary revisions.

There is nothing wrong with our being a bit selfish and assigning topics in which we are interested, or documents for which we have a need. Last semester, students in my technical writing class needed instructions to learn how to import charts and graphs from a graphics program to a word-processing program. I assigned the students in my class on writing software documentation to draft the instructions for importing the files. The students completed the documentation just as my technical writing class needed to create the graphics. Thus, my documentation students had worked on a real project with a real audience and purpose.

An almost infinite number of activities can be assigned that allow you to learn from your students. For example, in a unit on writing instructions, you might ask your students to explain how to use a tool to do something in their field, or in a unit on oral presentations, you might ask them to develop a poster about some aspect of a field in which they're interested. I've received instructions for constructing scaffolding, making golf clubs, and using a telescope, and I've viewed posters on fashion modeling, safety equipment at a manufacturing plant, and the St. Louis arch. I learned about each of these topics from my students, while my students learned how to create an effective report and poster from me.

This reciprocal learning occurs at other levels. Because modeling is one of the most influential methods for teaching students how to process knowledge, students who perceive their teachers as active learners, writers, and collaborators, are likely to adapt similar behavior patterns. Thus, by collaborating with students to solve problems and improve written discourse, we are establishing behavior patterns for engaging in teamwork and for using heuristics that we want our students to imitate. Brooks and Brooks (1993) confirm this:

> When students work with adults who continue to view themselves as learners, who ask questions with which they, themselves, grapple, who are willing and able to alter both content and practices in the pursuit of meaning and who treat students and their endeavors as works in progress, not finished products, students are more likely to demonstrate these characteristics themselves...Such teacher role models...honor students as emerging thinkers. (10)

Collaborating with Other Teachers

Several years ago I taught technical writing to a class of students who were enrolled in an Associate degree program in automotive technology at Illinois Central College (ICC). The students were disinterested, seldom turned their papers in on time if they turned them in at all, and rebelled at revising anything. They couldn't see the relevance of the course to their major and assured me that they would *never* need to write when they got a job in their chosen field. It became increasingly evident that unless I tied my assignments to projects on which the students were working in their automotive courses, I would never convince them that, indeed, they would write in the workplace. So I began discussing the possibility of collaborating on a course with a member of the automotive faculty. However, we never got past the discussion stage.

Designing a Poster Project

This year, my first year at Purdue Calumet, I decided to stop talking and *do* something. I went looking for someone with whom I could collaborate.

I found Roy Evans, a faculty member in the construction technology department who had been introduced to "process education" during the previous year, and had been looking for someone with whom he could share experiences as he implemented the various methods in his classroom. Our interest in each other's work was mutual. For my part, I was looking forward to learning about construction technology, and to finding out the kinds of courses that are taught in this field. I was about to learn a lot.

We had a total of three two-hour meetings, which were devoted to planning the joint project, determining the information students would need to complete the activity successfully, and developing a schedule for the lessons and various assignments respectively. During our first meeting, we brainstormed the types of writing the students would do once they were on the job. We talked about their need to write and read performance specifications and to draft materials and soil testing reports. I learned they would be responsible for writing responses to OSHA and submitting progress reports. We discussed the many audiences with whom they would correspond—general contractors, subcontractors, architects, engineers, financial organizations, and building owners. We considered a variety of projects. In the end we decided on posters.

Roy had been noticing an increasing number of poster sessions at the various conferences he had been attending and so had I. I liked the idea because it allowed me to integrate several aspects of the language arts—oral presentations and visualization—into a single unit. It also provided me with a valid reason to introduce computer graphics.

With that settled, we needed to determine a purpose for the posters so that we could write a prompt. Roy suggested that since many of the students were directly out of high school, the goal of the assignment should be to expand their knowledge of the field. He suggested that students write about a topic related to construction technology that he would not have sufficient time to discuss thoroughly during the course. Thus, their purpose would be to inform each other about an aspect of the field, and they would become each others' audience. The idea sounded good to me, and since Roy was the content area specialist, I was more than willing to follow his lead in this.

But I wasn't satisfied with limiting the writing assignments to posters. I felt that there were a number of additional writing assignments that could be integrated into this activity, i.e., a request memo proposing a topic, a progress report written about halfway through the project, and a written information report accompanying the posters, allowing me to introduce students to three more types of documents in an integrated approach. Roy was quite willing to go along. We decided to require students to turn in two copies of each document, one to me and one to Roy. However, we thought we should evaluate and grade the students' work separately, since we had different reasons for reading and requiring the documents. I planned to grade each written document based on its discourse features, while Roy decided to grade only the final report and poster based on the content. Rather than grade the response memo and the progress report, he wanted to respond in the same way a supervisor on a job would respond. He would simply approve or refuse to approve the idea proposed in the request memo, and by using the progress report, he would ascertain whether students needed assistance to meet their deadline or to develop an effective presentation.

Once we had settled on a major assignment, we needed to consider the kinds of information students would be required to know in order to fulfill it. We felt it was important they understand how and why posters are used, and the criteria for creating effective posters. We each did a search of the literature in our respective fields, and then shared the small amount of information we had found by duplicating whatever material was relevant and sending it through intercampus mail. Since little had been written about this genre, we devoted our second meeting to brainstorming. We came up with five situations in which posters would serve as an effective medium of communication. We also worked on developing a list of criteria for an effective poster. However, since neither one of us had any expertise in this area, nor had we found much information related to it, we felt we needed additional help and turned to the Office of University Relations, where one of the staff members, Debbie Rybecki, had been creating posters for several years. Thus, our collaborative circle was expanded. Our meeting with Debbie was conducted over the telephone.

At our next meeting, we developed a schedule for the lessons and assignments, and parceled out the lessons that each of us would be responsible for teaching. We agreed that everything should revolve around the content area, and that all lectures should be presented during Roy's class. During the first session, we decided Roy should introduce the assignment, speak about the content requirements, and display several models of good posters. We felt I should follow with the second presentation, discussing the context in which posters are used. Debbie would make the third presentation, explaining and illustrating the parameters for creating effective posters. After that, the students would work in my class drafting, peer conferencing, and revising their work. Over the course of the project, it was determined that I would assign and present the conventions for writing the additional three documents. After these decisions were made, we communicated by E-mail and voice mail, keeping each other informed of concerns students were having in relation to obtaining information, or developing their posters and meeting schedules. When I realized I was running behind schedule because of an unexpected conference I had to attend, I notified Roy and he adapted his schedule accordingly. When Roy realized he had to move up the deadline for the poster presentation, I scrambled to get the students ready.

Roy and I didn't get together again until the final day, when the students hung their posters along the walls in the building where Roy's classes were held. I walked along the corridor, watching the students help each other hang their work and then *read* the posters, pausing periodically to ask questions about a certain piece of information. They discussed their topics animatedly and knowledgeably. Only one poster had an error. During the preceding classes, the students had shared the documents that they planned to paste on their posters with several of their peers, requesting feedback and asking that errors be caught. And then they had revised. And revised again. And again. They had been acutely aware that a real audience would view their work. They knew that their posters would be hung along the hall, where not only their classmates but all the students majoring in Engineering and Technology would see their work. The assignment had virtually eliminated the quandary, perceived by Ede and Lunsford (1984), in which students are asked to perceive a simulated audience though they know that in reality that audience is the teacher in the role of evaluator. Although they were aware of the teacher's role, they were also aware of their other audiences, whose opinions of their work may have superceded those of their teacher's in terms of personal importance.

Results of a Collaborative Experience

As a result, my collaboration with Roy truly enriched all of those involved—teachers and students alike. Students were motivated; they collaborated and revised. Their evaluations were positive and exuberant. They were almost unanimous in claiming that they had learned new content, and would recommend that future classes engage in similar assignments. I, too, learned a lot. I learned about a variety of topics in construction technology, for which I had no knowledge prior to this class, and my knowledge of poster presentations was enhanced. Both Roy and I continue to use the activity, and now other members of the faculty are doing so also. The project did not take a great deal more of my time than a project on which I would have worked on my own. Gains in knowledge and in my teaching effectiveness were well worth whatever additional time I had devoted to the project.

I also gained a professional friend. Shortly after the class, Roy invited me to participate in a university-wide demonstration of projects involving technology in the classroom, and I invited him to join me in a presentation of our poster project at the NCTE spring conference.

The results of an integrated curriculum are limited only by our own imaginations. In one school, teachers in English and construction technology have engaged in parallel collaboration to teach Shakespeare. During English period, students read *Romeo and Juliet*; during technology class, they work on constructing a replica of the Globe theater.

In an anatomy and physiology class at a California Academy, students study health problems in various occupational fields. Then they write a report on their findings in conjunction with an English class. One student, after interviewing a worker in a frozen foods factory, investigated the problem of respiratory infections for employees working under these conditions. The student concluded there was a relationship between sudden temperature changes and respiratory problems and wrote a report on these findings (O'Neil 1994).

A Youth Apprenticeship Program in an eastern state has developed a project on workplace safety that involves social studies, science, math, and English classes. In social studies, students study the 1911 Triangle Waist Company fire. In science, they learn the principles behind what firefighters call *lapping in* and other effects of fires in buildings, while in math they learn to calculate volume in order to understand the amount of air space per worker that is required by today's fire laws. Finally, they have an opportunity to study the blueprints for a local building, to determine whether or not it is adhering to present fire codes. They then write an evaluation report of the building (O'Neil 1994, 4).

These projects can satisfy our own need for learning new content areas, and for being creative as we develop new lessons. They can also provide us with a more satisfying teaching experience, as our students respond more positively to our instruction. In the anatomy and physiology class at the Oakland Health and Bioscience Academy in California, students must learn 160 different terms that are part of the discipline's vocabulary. Their teacher, David DeLeews comments, "Students who are academically behind are more motivated because the academics are placed in a real-life context...it's just not true that the kids with 'lower' academic skills can't do higher-order thinking and find it satisfying" (O'Neil 1994, 4).

Collaborating to Develop Authentic Integrated Assignments

My collaboration with Roy has convinced me that if I am to reach these students—if they are to perceive the relevancy of the documents that I am trying to teach them to read and write—then I must integrate my lessons with the vocational/technical courses in which they are enrolled. In Chapter 1 we discussed the need for students to understand how the content and skills they learn are related to their own world. However, we are all too aware that in a traditional English class, in which academic and literary writing and reading are emphasized, that this relationship is seldom overtly evident, and although many of us go to great lengths to find links to help students understand how the *Aeropagitica, The Scarlet Letter,* or *Walden* relate to their lives, few students believe us. It is only when they are actually involved outside the classroom, using the knowledge and skills that we have taught them, that they recognize the validity of our explanations. If we are to provide them with activities that will convince them of the relevance of the skills we are teaching, then we will need to work closely with vocational/technical faculty, collaborating with them to integrate our fields in meaningful ways.

Overcoming Fears, Developing Openness, Becoming Flexible

Throughout most of my career, I have been lucky enough to find colleagues whose ideas, enthusiasm, competence, and openness complement my own. It is to these people that I have turned for assistance in designing curriculums, instructing students, and drafting my ideas. My collaboration with them has enriched me.

Having successfully collaborated on manuscripts and curriculum development, I find I prefer working with others than alone. It's more educational, easier, and, frankly, more fun. However, if you have not engaged in a collaborative endeavor previously, working closely with others may create a high degree of anxiety. Before entering into a collaborative arrangement, you should determine whether a project is likely to improve with collaboration, and whether there is a person who has knowledge that complements yours with whom you would feel comfortable working.

Openness. Opening our doors and making room for others to share our space can be frightening. We are worried that they may take away something we hold important, that they may gain control, that they may perceive our weaknesses. Yet our weaknesses are all too evident in our failure to provide our students with the procedural and content knowledge they need.

It is essential to enter into a collaborative project open-mindedly, willing to see our own field through someone else's eyes, to consider our priorities in terms of someone else's ideas, and to expand our philosophy to embrace the subtleties of someone else's beliefs. Seeing our various goals, objectives, and activities in another perspective can give us new insights into their relative importance. If we enter into a collaborative endeavor with an open mind, we may recognize that some of the skills we have not been teaching are just as necessary as those we have, and that some may be even more important. We may also find that relinquishing control to someone with more knowledge and skill in certain areas—computer software, technical fields—may not only ease much of the stress we have been under, but allow us to concentrate in those areas where we excel and which we enjoy teaching.

Flexibility. Flexibility is essential. We need to be willing to accommodate the schedule of others, and to recognize the need for additional time that inevitably accompanies the institution of new projects, regardless of the amount already allotted.

Planning Collaborative Activities

Collaboration takes time, effort, and, above all, commitment. When a school in Illinois simultaneously instituted the eight-block curriculum and a combined Tech Prep/College Prep track, the English and math teachers decided to collaborate on a variety of projects. They received a grant for a two-week summer planning session. Figuring that the session would provide a good base for determining their curriculum, they decided they would only need to meet on a weekly basis during the term. They set aside a ninety-minute planning period for each Friday morning to review the week's progress and plan the following week. However, they discovered that they needed to meet far more often. As school programs, student problems, and hitches in their lessons occurred and needed to be ironed out, they found themselves arriving at school an hour early for daily planning sessions. To avoid this problem, when teachers at Reynoldsburg High School in Ohio implemented a Global Connections classroom, they were given two daily planning periods: one for group planning and one for individual work (Levak, Merryfield, and Wilson 1993).

Most of the time devoted to a collaborative activity should be spent at the beginning, during the planning phase. This phase needs to involve three major decisions:

1. a decision on the assignment itself—what it should be, its purpose, and related assignments
2. a decision on the information, skills, and strategies students need to engage in the assignment successfully—the new knowledge, skills, and strategies students will need to learn, the scope and sequence of the lessons, and dates for assignment deadlines
3. a decision on the evaluation—what should be evaluated and by whom, whether the evaluation should be formative or summative, and the form of the evaluation, i.e., pass/fail, grades, or narrative response, such as Roy provided for the progress report

These decisions should be made with the understanding that they are not engraved in granite and can be altered as circumstances arise. If we are flexible, then changes won't frustrate or inconvenience us too much, and we will be able to adapt our plans quickly and easily to new situations. Thus, after engaging in several collaborative endeavors, we should discover they are less time-consuming and threatening than we thought at first, and we should be far more willing to search out new content fields to integrate with our own, so that we can provide our students with relevant learning experiences.

Collaborating with Business, Industry, and Community Members

Both the health occupation class activity and the safety hazard class activity we discussed previously required collaboration among teachers of different content areas, but also between teachers and representatives of local government agencies and industries. Students in the health occupations course needed access to the frozen food factory, and students studying the fire laws needed blueprints of local buildings. By partnering with local agencies, businesses, and industries, we can provide our students with projects that truly reflect the workplace, rather than scenarios that represent our idea of what the workplace entails.

A partnership between ourselves and community institutions can assume many forms. In some cases, industries may be willing to provide us with curriculum materials. The Regional Airport Authority serving Louisville and Jefferson County, Kentucky, created a curriculum entitled "Aviation 2010." The materials include an activity requiring students to write up an itinerary for a rock band on an international tour. Students must learn to read flight schedules, to deal with negative numbers in relation to time zones as they fly the band from the United States to Japan, and to design and write an itinerary that allows busy travelers to locate the information they need easily and to read it quickly. The Airport Authority also developed the following activities, which can be integrated with a history class.

LESSON TITLE:	THE PLAY'S THE THING
	Language Arts, Social Studies, Sciences
SKILLS:	• identifies historical mysteries
	• creates imaginative answers for unanswered historical questions
	• dramatizes events
PERFORMANCE OBJECTIVES:	• The student will conduct research on a historical "mystery."
	• The student will write a one-act play dramatizing what the student concludes might have happened.
MATERIALS:	Library resources
PROCEDURE:	1. Ask the class what happened to Amelia Earhart or to the fighter squadron that vanished in the Bermuda Triangle. News articles can be used on the latter.
	2. Divide the class into production groups, and have each pick a "mystery"—e.g., What happened to Amelia Earhart? What happened to Will Rogers? What happened to the fighters?
	3. Have each group research the event, and write a one-act play solving the mystery. Groups can then present or read their plays to the rest of the class.

Many businesses are opening their doors for students to observe how information is communicated. Businesses may also provide blueprints and other documents to serve as examples of the kinds of written communication that occur, or representatives from businesses may visit schools to make presentations on the kinds of reading and writing in which they engage in their work. In Norfolk, Virginia, several persons from engineering firms made presentations about the engineering/technical design field to students at Maury High School. Students and teachers alike discovered the importance of good communication skills when they learned that in order for these consulting companies to be hired for a job or project, their employees had to write proposals to do the engineering work.

Many businesses offer internships, apprenticeships, and cooperative arrangements that allow students to actually work and learn on the job, providing them with opportunities to learn how to communicate workplace information.

Learning about the workplace is no longer limited to our students. Businesses are also opening their doors to teachers to help them understand the kinds of skills students need to enter the workforce. Opportunities for shadowing are being made available, allowing us to follow an employee at her work to discover the kinds of communication in which she engages. Eight English teachers in the Norfolk, Virginia, schools spent part of their vacations shadowing employees at nearby plants and offices. Amazed at the variety of different types of writing tasks employees were required to do, they returned from their experiences with piles of authentic writing tasks that included public relations materials, brochures, application forms, proposals, technical reports, documented research, and proposal abstracts. Additionally, the teachers discovered the importance of oral communication in engineering fields, having heard stories about employees who were not promoted because they lacked good communication skills. They also saw the high level of technical reading required for the various jobs in the field (Hosay 1996).

Businesses are also providing externships, which allow teachers to work for a summer or a semester in an industry to gain experience in the workplace outside of academia.

Maintaining Our Integrity

Despite these positive experiences with business partnerships, business involvement in schools is often viewed apprehensively. Critics see it as self-serving. Neil Postman warns that businesses are trying to take over the schools, and that we need to guard against training our students for what business wants (1995). However, if in fearing domination by industry, we withhold from our students the skills and knowledge they need to become useful citizens, we are failing to fulfill our responsibilities to them. Educating our children to be able to assume productive work in society is as much a part of our mandate as is our charge to provide our children with an aesthetic appreciation of the arts. We need the members of business and industry to *help* us determine the knowledge and skills our students must master for the workplace as well as to provide knowledge, skills, and materials to instruct our students effectively. Rather than refuse to collaborate with business and industry, and thereby prevent our students from obtaining the education they deserve, we should take steps to assure that corporations cannot gain control of our classrooms.

Conclusion

In summing up the collaborative effort between teachers at Maury High School in Norfolk, Virginia, and local businesses, Jane Hosay, the Director of Vocational Education for the state of Virginia and a former English teacher, comments:

> As a result of this project, students and teachers see connections among the disciplines, instructional activities in the vocational classes have been upgraded, instructional activities in the English classroom include some real-world application, and teachers and students have gained first-hand knowledge of communication skills requirements in the workplace. Many employers have said to me, "Send me an English teacher. I would like to share information about the reading, writing, speaking, and listening skills required in our company."
>
> What we do as English teachers matters more than we know. (1996, 3)

Epilogue

As I wait for the last chapter of this book to come off my printer, I clear the coffee table in my living room so that I can lay out the manuscript and the artwork that will accompany it. I carefully transport a large piece of pottery from the far left corner of the table where it sits to a place of safety on a shelf in my bookcase. It is a deep teal blue teapot with a convoluted handle that bears a striking resemblance to Aladdin's lamp. We bought it from a student who was showing his works at Sangamon State University's Senior Art show. We had become acquainted with Brent Morris several summers before, when he painted the outside of our windows. The paint that had been on the frames, at least five layers deep, had already started peeling when we finally hired Brent. He worked on those windows as conscientiously as he must have worked on the teapot, scraping off the old paint, sanding down the wood, putting on the primer, then laying on coat after coat of paint. After he was through with the job, he came back to visit us periodically, to have lunch, talk, and check on the paint. Was it wearing okay? Were there any places he needed to go back over? No, we said, knowing if there were, he would take care of them.

House painter or artistic sculptor, Brent cared about what he did. He had learned the importance of quality, regardless of whether he was working on the functional windows of a house or the intricate carvings for the handle of a teapot that was to decorate a coffee table.

It is this feeling of pride in what they have done, this recognition of the quality of their work, regardless of whether that work is an algebraic equation with two unknowns or a bookcase, with which we need to engender our students. We can do that by respecting them and their work.

Lerner (1996) claims, "Work [is] the activity through which we are able to externalize ourselves in the world and act together toward shared goals" (220). He goes on to say that it is not that work "is always easy or always fun but that it makes sense to us. It makes us feel connected to others, and to a larger ethical and spiritual purpose" (249). Reflecting Pirsig's ethos, he concludes "One aspect of responsibility is that people must do a good job. If we care for others and

143

understand how our work is needed by them, then we must commit ourselves by doing our best" (250).

As teachers, we can prepare our students to find similar self-fulfillment, to become the caring workers Lerner forecasts, by providing them with training in the skills they need. In so doing, we can gain pride in our own work and fulfill ourselves.

References

Ackerman, David, and D. N. Perkins. 1989. "Integrating Thinking and Learning Skills Across the Curriculum." In *Interdisciplinary Curriculum: Design and Implementation*, edited by Heidi Hayes Jacob, 77–96. Alexandria, VA: Association of Supervision and Curriculum Development.

Agricola, Georgius. 1950. *De Re Metallica*. Translated by Herbert Clark Hoover and Lou Henry Hoover. New York: Dover Publications.

Applebee, Arthur. 1992. "The Background for Reform." In *Literature Instruction: A Focus on Student Response*, edited by Judith Langer, 1–18. Urbana, IL: National Council of Teachers of English.

———. 1990. "Fostering Literary Understanding: The State of the Schools." In *Transactions with Literature*, edited by Edmund Farrell and James Squire, 59–64. Urbana,IL: National Council of Teachers of English.

Armstrong, Thomas. 1994. *Multiple Intelligences in the Classroom*. Alexandria, VA: Association of Supervision and Curriculum Development.

Ayers, Chesley. 1975. *Specifications for Architecture, Engineering, and Construction*. New York: McGraw Hill.

Beach, Richard. 1990. "New Directions on Research in Response in Literature." In *Transactions with Literature*, edited by Edmund Farrell and James Squire, 65–78. Urbana, IL: National Council of Teachers of English.

Betts, Frank. 1994. "On the Birth of the Communication Age: A Converstation with David Thornburg." *Educational Leadership* 51: 20–23.

Bishop, John J. 1992. "Why U. S. Students Need Incentives to Learn." *Educational Leadership* 49: 15–18.

Blicq, Ron. 1994. "Technical Communication in the High Schools." *STC E&R Link* 3: 8–9.

Bloom, Benjamin. 1981. *All Our Children Learning*. New York: McGraw Hill.

Boiarsky, Carolyn. 1991. "Fluency, Fluidity, and Word Processing." *Journal of Advanced Composition* 11: 123–34.

Boiarsky, Carolyn, and Margot Soven. 1995. *Writings from the Workplace*. Boston: Allyn and Bacon.

Bonstingl, John Jay. 1992. "The Total Quality Classroom." *Educational Leadership* 49: 66–70.

Bouyea, Bob. 1993. "Will Cat Bring Team Concept to Peoria?" *Peoria Journal Star* (Sept. 14): A5.

Brandt, Ron. 1990. "On Learning Styles: A Conversation with Pat Guild." *Educational Leadership* 48: 10–13.

———. 1989/90. "On Cooperative Learning: A Conversation with Spencer Kagan." *Educational Leadership* 47: 8–11.

Brooks, Jacqueline Grennon, and Martin G. Brooks. 1993. *The Case for Constructivist Classrooms.* Alexandria, VA: Association for Supervision and Curriculum Development.

Bruce, Dan. 1987. "Toxic Shock Syndrome: Back to the Future." *Journal of the American Medical Association* 257 (8) [27 February]: 1094–95.

Bundy, Diana. 1993. "The Computer and the Family History Project." *English Journal* 82: 69–70.

Byrne, Sandra M., Anne Constant, and Gary Moore. 1992. "Making Transitions from School to Work." *Educational Leadership* 49: 23–26.

Caine, Renate, and Geoffrey Caine. 1991. *Making Connections: Teaching and the Human Brain.* Alexandria, VA: Association for Supervision and Curriculum Development.

Calkins, Lucy McDormick. 1980. "Research Update: When Children Want to Punctuate: Basic Skills Belong in Context." *Language Arts* 57: 567–73.

Campione, Joseph C. 1987. "Metacognitive Components of Instructional Research with Problem Learners." In *Metacognition, Motivation, and Understanding,* edited by Franz E. Weinert and Rainer H. Kluew. Hillsdale, NJ: Erlbaum.

Carbo, Marie. 1990. "Igniting the Literary Revolution Through Reading Styles." *Educational Leadership* 48: 26–31.

Carlson, G. Robert, and Anne Sherrill. 1988. *Voices of Readers.* Urbana, IL: National Council of Teachers of English.

Clancy, Tom. 1984. *The Hunt for Red October.* New York: Berkley Books.

Commission on the Skills of the American Workforce. 1990. *America's Choice: High Skills or Low Wages.* Rochester, NY: National Center on Education and the Economy.

Costanzo, William. 1994. "Reading, Writing, and Thinking in an Age of Electronic Literacy." In *Literacy and Computers,* edited by Cynthia Selfe and Susan Hilligoss. New York: Modern Language of America.

Couture, Barbara, and Jane Rymer Goldstein. 1985. *Cases for Technical and Professional Writing.* Boston: Little, Brown.

Crichton, Michael. 1994a. *Disclosure.* New York: Knopf.

———. 1994b. "Letter to the Editor." *Atlantic Monthly* (Dec.): 14–15.

———. 1992. *Rising Sun.* New York: Ballantine Books.

Defoe, Daniel. [1722] 1969. *Journal of the Plague Year.* Oxford, England: Oxford University Press.

Deming, W. Edward. 1988. *Out of the Crisis.* Cambridge, MA: Massachusetts Institute of Technology Press.

Dewey, John. 1981. *The School and Society.* Carbondale, IL: Southern Illinois University Press.

Dickens, Charles. [1854] 1981. *Hard Times.* New York: Bantam Books.

DiPardo, Anne. 1996. "Seeking Alternatives: The Wisdom of Collaborative Teaching." *English Education* 28: 109–26.

Drake, Susan. 1993. *Planning Integrated Curriculum.* Alexandria, VA: Association of Supervision and Curriculum Development.

Dunn, Rita. 1990. "Rita Dunn Answers Questions on Learning Styles." *Educational Leadership* 48: 15–19.

Dwyer, David. 1994, "Apple Classrooms of Tomorrow: What We've Learned." *Educational Leadership* 51: 4–10.

Dyson, Anne. 1989. *Collaboration Through Writing and Reading: Exploring Possibilities.* Urbana, IL: National Council of Teachers of English.

Ede, Lisa, and Andrea Lunsford. 1984. "Audience Addressed/Audience Invoked." *College English* 35: 155–71.

Educational Research Service. 1995. Survey on student use of the Internet.

Eiseley, Loren. 1973. *Innocent Assassins.* New York: Scribner's & Sons.

Farrell, Edmund. 1990. Preface to *Transactions with Literature,* edited by Edmund Farrell and James Squire, vii–viii. Urbana, IL: National Council of Teachers of English.

Gagon, Roger. 1995. "Teaching WordPerfect in the Classroom." *WordPerfect DOS Magazine* 7: 32–38.

Gardner, Howard. 1997. Speech. *ABC News.* 21 May.

———. 1994. *Multiple Intelligences: Theory into Practice.* New York: Basic Books.

———. 1983. *Frames of Mind.* New York: Basic Books.

Greene, Maxine. 1991. "Teaching: The Question of Personal Reality." In *Staff Development for Education in the 90s: New Demands, New Realities, New Perspectives,* edited by A. Lieberman and L. Miller, 3–14. 2d ed. New York: Teachers College Press.

Hager, P. J., and R. J. Nelson. 1993. "Chaucer's 'A Treatise on the Astrolabe': A 600-year-old Model for Humanizing Technical Documents." *IEEE Transactions on Professional Communication* 36: 87–94.

Hailey, Arthur. 1971. *Wheels.* Garden City, NY: Doubleday.

Hanson, Amy. 1996. "Whatever Happened to the Traditional Resume: Preparing Students for an Electronic Job Search." *ATTW Newsletter* 6: 4–6.

Harris Education Research Center. 1991. "An Assessment of American Education: The View of Employers, Higher Educators, the Public, Recent Students, and Their Parents." Survey sponsored by the Committee for Economic Development. New York: Louis Harris and Associates.

Hirsch, E.D., Jr. 1987. *Cultural Literacy.* Boston: Houghton Mifflin.

Hoover, Herbert. 1952. *The Memoirs of Herbert Hoover.* London: Hollis and Carter.

Hosay, Jane. 1996. "Bringing Workplace English to the Classroom by Going Out to the Workplace." Report for Norfolk Public Schools Board of Education, Norfolk, VA.

Huckin, Thomas. 1983. "A Cognitive Approach to Readability." In *New Essays in Technical and Scientific Communication: Research, Theory, and Practice,* edited by Paul W. Anderson, John Brockman, and Carolyn R. Miller, 90–108. Farmingdale, NY: Baywood Publishing Co.

Hull, Dan. 1993. *Opening Minds, Opening Doors.* Waco, TX: Center for Occupational Research and Development.

Hyerle, David. 1996. *Visual Tools for Constructing Knowledge.* Alexandria, VA: Association for Supervision and Curriculum Development.

Hynds, Susan. 1992. "Challenging Questions in the Teaching of Literature." In *Literature Instruction: A Focus on Student Response,* edited by Judith Langer, 78–100. Urbana, IL: National Council of Teachers of English.

Jacobs, Heidi Hayes, ed. 1989. *Interdisciplinary Curriculum: Design and Implementation.* Alexandria, VA: Association for Supervision and Curriculum Development.

Jones, Beau Fly, et al. 1987. *Strategic Teaching and Learning: Cognitive Instruction in the Content Areas.* Alexandria, VA: Association for Supervision and Curriculum Development.

Kagan, Spencer. 1989/90. "The Structural Approach to Cooperative Learning." *Educational Leadership* 47: 12–16.

Katz, Lillian G. 1985. "Dispositions in Early Childhood Education." ERIC/EECE Clearinghouse. Bulletin 18: 2. Urbana, IL: ERIC Clearinghouse.

Kolb, David A. 1984. *Experiential Learning: Experience as the Source of Learning and Development.* New Jersey: Prentice Hall.

Langer, Judith. 1992. "Rethinking Literature Instruction." In *Literature Instruction: A Focus on Student Response,* edited by Judith Langer. Urbana, IL: National Council of Teachers of English.

Langland, William. 1966. *Piers the Ploughman.* Baltimore, MD: Penguin Books.

Lazarus, Arnold, and W. Wendell Smith. 1983. *A Glossary of Literature and Composition.* Urbana, IL: National Council of Teachers of English.

Lerner, Michael. 1996. *The Politics of Meaning.* Reading, MA: Addison-Wesley.

Leroy, Patricia. 1991. "Nontraditional Library Research." In *The English Classroom in the Computer Age,* edited by William Wresch. Urbana, IL: National Council of Teachers of English.

Levak, Barbara A., Merry M. Merryfield, and Robert C. Wilson. 1993. "Global Connections." *Educational Leadership* 48: 73–75.

Leyva, Ric. 1996. "*Of Mice and Men* Moves to Multimedia." *Peoria Journal Star* (March 10): B3.

Little, Judith Warren. 1990. "The Persistance of Privacy: Autonomy and Initiative in Teachers' Professional Relations." *Teachers College Record* 91: 509–36.

Magaziner, Ira, and Hillary Rodham Clinton. 1992. "Will America Choose High Skills or Low Wages?" *Educational Leadership* 49: 10–14.

Marzano, Robert J., et al. 1988. *Dimensions of Thinking: A Framework for Curriculum Instruction.* Alexandria, VA: Association for Supervision and Curriculum Development.

McCarthy, Bernice. 1990. "Using the 4MAT System to Bring Learning Styles to Schools." *Educational Leadership* 48: 31–36.

McKown, David, and A. Nauda. 1993. "The Brave New World of Professional Communication." *IEEE Professional Communication Society Newsletter* 37: 1.

Means, Barbara, and Kerry Olson. 1994. "The Link Between Technology and Authentic Learning." *Educational Leadership* 51: 15–18.

Melville, Herman. [1851] 1983. *Moby Dick.* New York: The Library of America.

Moffett, James, and Betty Jane Wagner. 1992. *Student Centered Language Arts, K–12.* Portsmouth, NH: Boynton/Cook.

Morics, Catherine. 1991. "Autobiographical Newspapers." In *English Classrooms in the Computer Age,* edited by William Wresch, 109–113. Urbana, IL: National Council of Teachers of English.

Muir, Mike. 1994. "Putting Computer Projets at the Heart of the Curriculum." *Educational Leadership* 51: 30–32.

National Research Council. 1994. *Preparing for the Workplace: Charting a Course for Federal Postsecondary Training Policy.* Washington, DC: National Academy Press.

Nelms, Ben. 1988. "Sowing the Dragon's Teeth: An Introduction in the First Person." In *Literature in the Classroom: Readers, Texts, and Contexts,* edited by Ben Nelms. Urbana, IL: National Council of Teachers of English.

Norris, Frank. [1901] 1986. *The Octopus.* New York: Penguin Books.

North Central Regional Educational Laboratory. 1994. "Blueprint for Technical Assistance and Training Model for Illinois Project Success." Unpublished paper. Oak Brook Park, IL: North Central Regional Educational Laboratory.

Olsen, Gary. 1991. "Eideteker: The Professional Communicator in the New Visual Culture." *IEEE Transactions on Professional Communication* 24: 13–19.

O'Neil, John. 1994a. "Preparing Students for Work." *Update* 36 (9): 4–5.

———. 1994b. "Getting a Head Start on a Career." *Update* 36 (9): 1, 3–4.

———. 1992a. "Preparing for the Changing Workplace." *Educational Leadership* 49: 6–9.

———. 1992b. "On Education and the Economy: A Conversation with Marc Tucker." *Educational Leadership* 49: 19–22.

———. 1990. "Making Sense of Style." *Educational Leadership* 48:4–9.

Packer, Arnold, H. 1992. "Taking Action on the SCANS Report." *Educational Leadership* 49: 27–31.

Pauly, Edwards, Hillary Kopp, and Joshua Haimson. 1995. *Homegrown Lessons.* San Francisco: Jossey Bass.

Peck, Kyle L., and Denise Dorricott. 1994. "Why Use Technology?" *Educational Leadership* 51: 11–14.

Phelan, Patricia. 1990. *Literature and Life*. Urbana, IL: National Council of Teachers of English.

Pirsig, Robert M. 1976. *Zen and the Art of Motorcycle Maintenance*. New York: Bantam Books.

Pollio, Marcus Vitruvius. 1960. *The Ten Books of Architecture*. Translated by Morris Hickey Morgan. London: Dover Publications.

Postman, Neil. 1995. *The End of Educaton*. New York: Vintage Books.

Probst, Robert. 1992. "Five Kinds of Literary Knowing." In *Literature Instruction: A Focus on Student Response*, edited by Judith Langer, 54–77. Urbana, IL: National Council of Teachers of English.

———. 1990. "Literature as Exploration and the Classroom." In *Transactions with Literature*, edited by Edmund Farrell and James Squire, 27–38. Urbana, IL: National Council of Teachers of English.

———. 1988. *Response and Analysis: Teaching Literature in Junior and Senior High School*. Portsmouth, NH: Boynton/Cook.

Purves, Alan. 1992. "Testing Literature." In *Literature Instruction: A Focus on Student Response*, edited by Judith Langer, 19–34. Urbana, IL: National Council of Teachers of English.

———. 1990. "Can Literature Be Rescued from Reading?" In *Transactions with Literature*, edited by Edmund Farrell and James Squire, 79–96. Urbana, IL: National Council of Teachers of English.

Reddick, Randy, and Elliot King. 1996. *The Online Student: Making the Grade on the Internet*. Fort Worth: Harcourt Brace College Publishers.

Robert, Henry M. [1876] 1990. *Robert's Rules of Order*. Ninth edition. Chicago: Scott Foresman.

Roos, Frank J. 1954. *An Illustrated Book of Art History*. New York: Macmillan.

Rosenblatt, Louise. 1978. *The Reader, the Text, the Poem: The Transactional Theory of the Literary Work*. Carbondale, IL: Southern Illinois University Press.

———. 1938. *Literature as Exploration*. New York: D. Appleton Century.

Rosenholtz, S. 1985. *Teachers' Workplace: The Social Organization of Schools*. New York: Teachers College Press.

Ross, James. 1991. "Autobiographical Newspapers as Introductions to Journalism." In *The English Classroom in the Computer Age*, edited by William Wresch, 113–117. Urbana, IL: National Council of Teachers of English.

Rubin, Bryndis. 1994. "The Internet: Where Few Trainers Have Gone Before." *Training and Development*: 25–30.

Secretary's Commission on Achieving Necessary Skills [SCANS]. 1991. *What Work Requires of Schools: A SCANS Report for America 2000*. Washington, DC: U. S. Department of Labor.

Sharan, Yael, and Shlomo Sharan. 1989/90. "Group Investigation Expands Cooperative Learning." *Educational Leadership* 47: 17–21.

Sheppard, Nathaniel. 1996. "Finding a College on the Net." *Chicago Tribune* (April 2): 1–6.

Sinclair, Upton. [1906] 1985. *The Jungle*. New York: Penguin Books.

Smith, Frank. 1984. "Reading Like a Writer." In *Composing and Comprehending*, edited by Julie Jensen. Urbana, IL: National Council of Teachers of English.

Starr, Kevin. 1986. Introduction to *The Octopus*, by Frank Norris. New York: Penguin Books.

Stern, David, Neal Finkelstein, James R. Stone III, John Latting, et al. 1995. *School to Work: Research on Programs in the United States*. Bristol, PA: Falmer Press.

Taggert, Linda. 1994. "Student Autobiographies with a Twist of Technology." *Educational Leadership* 51: 34–35.

Tebeaux, Elizabeth. 1993. "From Orality to Textuality in English Accounting and Its Books, 1553–1680: The Power of Visual Presentation." *Journal of Business and Technical Communication* 7: 322–59.

———. 1992. "Renaissance Epistolography and the Origins of Business Correspondence, 1568–1640: Implications for Modern Pedagogy." *Journal of Business and Technical Communication* 6: 75–98.

Tebeaux, Elizabeth, and Mary Lay. 1992. "Women in Technical Books from the Renaissance." *IEEE Transactions on Professional Communication* 35: 197–206.

Thucydides. 1934. "The Plague of Athens." In *The Complete Writings*. New York: Random House.

Verne, Jules. [1873] 1993. *Twenty Thousand Leagues Under the Sea*. Stamford, CT: Longmeadow Press.

Whitmore, Joanne Rand. 1980. *Giftedness, Conflict, and Underachievement*. Boston: Allyn & Bacon.

Wresch, William. 1991. *The English Classroom in the Computer Age: Thirty Lesson Plans*. Urbana, IL: National Council of Teachers of English.